50
SIMPLE
THINGS
KIDS CAN
DO TO
SAVE THE
EARTH

The EarthWorks Group

Illustrations by Michele Montez

Andrews and McMeel
A Universal Press Syndicate Company
Kansas City • New York

This is for all kids, but especially
Rocky, Gideon, Sam, and Joshua

THIS BOOK IS PRINTED ON RECYCLED PAPER.

Created and Packaged by Javnarama
Designed by Javnarama
Layout by Fritz Springmeyer
Illustrations by Michele Montez

We've provided a great deal of information about
practices and products in our book. In most cases,
we've relied on advice, recommendations, and research
by others whose judgments we consider accurate and
free from bias. However, we can't and don't guarantee
the results. This book offers you a start.
The responsibility for using it
ultimately rests with you.

ISBN 0-8362-2301-2
Library of Congress Catalog Card Number: 90-34753
First Edition 10 9 8 7 6 5 4 3 2 1

ACKNOWLEDGMENTS

John Javna and the EarthWorks Group would like to thank everyone who helped make this book possible, including:

- Fritz Springmeyer
- Michele Montez
- Phil Catalfo
- Linda Glaser
- Anne Grant
- Gil Friend
- Julie Bennett
- Jackie Kaufman
- Randi Hacker
- Robin Dellabough
- Kim Raftery
- Kevin Raftery
- Chris Calwell
- The Natural Resources Defense Council
- Karina Lutz, *Home Energy* magazine
- Pamela Lichtman
- Andy Sohn
- Susan Fassberg
- King Hempel
- Marydele Donnelly, Center for Marine Conservation
- Lori Wright
- Mary Robinson
- John Schindel
- Jean Miller
- Gina Pardeaux
- Kamille
- Michael Nash
- Harriot Manley
- Gideon Javna
- Tom Thornton
- Kathleen Andrews
- Lisa Shadid
- Dorothy O'Brien
- Donna Martin
- Jessamine Catalfo
- Lisa Epstein, and the entire fifth grade class at John Muir Elementary School, Berkeley, California
- Hope DeMarco
- Jesse Hornstein
- Regan Horner
- Emika Porter
- Joey Leichter
- Maya Crayton
- David Moser
- Shannon Lemmons
- Shiquela Smith
- Karen Leason
- Lauren Weber
- Adam Adler
- Shannon Prichard
- Ryan Prichard
- Gabriel Catalfo
- John McGovern
- Damien DeMarco
- Adriana DeMarco
- Bryn Kahn
- Claire Barrett-Liu

"When I die I would like to give the next generation a better Earth than I had."—*Joey Leichter, Age 10*

CONTENTS

SPREADING THE WORD

ECO-EXPERIMENTS

A NOTE TO KIDS

This book is for you.
You can do anything you want with it.
You can sleep with it.
You can sit on it.
You can balance it on your head.
Of course, I hope you read it. But that's just me.

Here's what I've been thinking about: I was talking to my friend
Gideon the other day—he's nine years old—and he said something surprising.

    I asked him if he thought kids could save the Earth. He an-
swered, "Well...umm...I don't know."

    I was hoping he'd say, "Yeah, you bet!"

    I guess a lot of kids don't really think they can make a big
difference in saving the Earth. They think they don't have the
power.

    But they're wrong.

    Kids have a *lot* of power. Whenever you say something,
grown-ups *have* to listen. Whenever you care about something,
grown-ups have to care, too. Whenever you do something,
grown-ups have to pay attention. They don't always tell you this,
but it's true. So if saving the Earth is important to you, then
grown-ups will have to follow along.

    This book is full of things you can do to help protect our
planet. A lot of them are fun. Some take work. Some give you a
chance to teach your parents, instead of the other way around.
But all of them will show you that you *can* make a difference.
And *that* is the power to save the Earth.

    Have fun!

            Your friend,

            John Javna

TO PARENTS AND TEACHERS

As you probably realize from firsthand experience, today's adults have so much trouble overcoming our bad habits that we find it tough to accomplish even the simplest of things. Recycling, conserving water and energy, and car-pooling are easy tasks that are obviously good for the Earth. But because they're unfamiliar to us, we struggle with them.

Today's kids don't have that luxury. When they grow up, the little things will *have* to be second-nature to them, be-cause they'll be tackling—and hopefully, solving—the enormous issues we only talk about: global warming, water pollution, acid rain, the ozone hole, and so on.

KID POWER
In our experience, kids are not only willing, but very eager to do their part. But they need information, encourage-ment, and—this is the important one—the sense that they have the power to make a difference.

50 Simple Things Kids Can Do is really about empowering our children. Right now, we run the risk of letting them grow up feeling that the environmental problems we—and they—face are too big, too difficult, too hopeless to deal with.

We can't let that happen!

Children must be told, and shown, that they can accomplish wonderful things for the Earth. They have to experience the feeling of satisfaction that goes with doing something right and good.

This is our responsibility as their parents and teachers. If we accomplish nothing else in our lives, we must provide them with the tools for survival. And in the 1990s, that means giving them the confidence that they can change —and save—the world.

As I write this, my wife Sharon and I are expecting our first child. The due date is about two weeks away. So this book has a special meaning to me. It is a gift to our child—a gift of hope and, I believe, a future. It is a gift I know that each of you want to give to your own children.

We can do it.

John Javna
The EarthWorks Group
March 13, 1990

WHAT'S

HAPPENING

ACID RAIN

UP IN THE SKY
When we look up, we see the clouds and the blue sky. But there are other things in the sky that we don't see. Some of these are harmful to the Earth.

WHAT HAPPENS
When power plants burn coal to make electricity, and when cars burn gasoline, invisible gases are released into the air. Some of these gases can mix with water and make it *acidic*, like lemon juice or vinegar.

WHAT CAN HAPPEN
Sometimes the gases get into rain clouds, where they get mixed in with rain or snow. Then the acid falls back to earth with the rain or snow. This is called acid rain.

BAD NEWS
Acid rain is extremely harmful to plants, rivers and lakes, and the creatures that live in them.

In some places it is killing forests. And it pollutes the water that animals and people need to drink.

OUR MISSION
It's very important for us to stop making acid rain. One good way to do that is to drive our cars less. Another good way is to save energy. The less energy we use, the less coal those power plants will have to burn.

You and your family can save energy in lots of ways. Saving energy means saving the Earth. To find out more about what you can do, turn to *Spending Energy Wisely*.

AIR POLLUTION

THE BROWN STUFF
Many cities around the world have air filled with a pollution called "smog." This is so strong in some places that the air, which should be a beautiful blue, actually looks brown.

THE OLD DAYS
Until about 150 years ago, the air was pure and clean—perfect for the people and animals of the earth to breathe.

FACTORIES
Then people started building factories. Those factories and many of the things they make, like cars, put a lot of harmful gases into the air. Then people started driving cars, which added more pollution to the air.

TODAY
Today the air is so polluted in some places that it's not always safe to breathe!

DOWN WITH POLLUTION!
Polluted air is not only bad for people and animals, but for trees and other plants, as well. And in some places it's even damaging farmers' crops—the food we eat. So it's very important for us to "clean up our act," and clean up the air we all breathe.

Everyone can help keep our air clean and safe. It's even fun! You can plant a tree, ride your bike, and even write a letter to a newspaper. For more ideas on how to clean up our air, keep reading!

DISAPPEARING ANIMALS

THE PEOPLE BOOM
Every day, there are more and more people living on Earth. All these people need room to live. So they move into places that are already homes for plants and animals. Forests are cut down, and wild areas are filled with houses and stores.

WHAT HAPPENS
When people move into new land, the plants and animals that live there can become *endangered*—which means that because there's no place for them to live, they begin to disappear. Some even become *extinct*—which means that they all die out, and are gone from the Earth forever.

WHAT CAN HAPPEN
We enjoy pictures and stories about the dinosaurs who lived on the earth many millions of years ago. They're all *extinct now*. That could

happen to elephants, zebras, redwood trees, frogs, butterflies, robins, or goldfish...or other animals, if we're not careful.

OUR MISSION
Let's keep the Earth green and healthy and full of millions of wonderful creatures!

Can you help animals? Yes! To find out how, check out *Preserving Our Oceans, Rivers, Lakes, and Streams, Protecting Animals,* and *Keeping the Earth Green.*

TOO MUCH GARBAGE!

GARBAGE AWAY!
When you throw something away, it goes in a garbage can. Once a week the garbage truck comes and the can is emptied, and that's the last you see of it. But what do you think happens to the garbage then? Does it just disappear? No way!

WHAT HAPPENS
Almost all garbage is taken to a garbage dump, or *landfill*, where the garbage truck empties it onto the ground. After the truck leaves, a big tractor comes along and pushes dirt on top of the garbage. So, most of our garbage is just buried.

THE BIG MESS
Now we are making so much garbage that in many places, there is not enough room to bury it all.

OUR MISSION
We have to act fast and cut down the amount of garbage we make. Can we do it? You bet!

HERE'S HOW
We can recycle (which means re-using materials instead of throwing them away) and precycle (which means not buying things that can't be re-used, like plastic wrapping and other packaging.) If we recycle and precycle we will produce a lot less garbage, and help keep our planet green!

Recycling and precycling projects can be lots of fun. To find out more about what you can do, see *Guarding Our Buried Treasures*, and *Be a Paper-Saver*.

THE GREENHOUSE EFFECT

A GREENHOUSE?
A greenhouse is a building made of glass, where you can grow flowers and other plants that need a lot of warmth.

HOW IT WORKS
The sun shines in through the glass and warms the greenhouse, and the roof and walls keep the heat from getting out.

OUR GREENHOUSE
The Earth is surrounded by a blanket of invisible gases (with names like *carbon dioxide*) that act just like a greenhouse. The sun shines in, and the blanket of gases traps the heat like a roof, keeping it close to the planet. That's good—we can't live without warmth.

WHAT'S GOING ON
Factories, electric power plants, and cars are making a lot of new gases. Even trees, when they're cut down, give off the gases! These new gases are trapping more and more of the sun's heat. This is called the *greenhouse effect*, or *global warming*.

WHAT CAN HAPPEN
If the earth's temperature gets hotter by just a few degrees, it could change the weather all over the planet in big ways. Places that are warm would become too hot to live in, and places that are cold would become warm. The places that grow most of our food could get too hot to grow crops anymore.

Every kid can help stop the greenhouse effect by using less energy, protecting and planting trees, and by recycling so factories don't need to work as hard making things. This book is full of tips on how to do it!

THE OZONE HOLE

THE OZONE LAYER

Up in the sky, above the air we breathe, there's a layer of gas called ozone. It helps us by blocking out rays from the sun that can harm our skin, and by letting the rays that are good for us come through. We're lucky to have the ozone to protect us!

WHAT'S HAPPENING

Now the ozone layer is being damaged by gases that people have made. The gases are called CFCs, and halons. They are used in refrigerators, fire extinguishers, air conditioners, plastic foam, and some other things.

HOW IT HAPPENS

The CFCs float up to the top of the atmosphere, where the layer of ozone is, and "eat up" the ozone just like little Pac-Men.

OUR MISSION

Scientists are very concerned about the ozone layer, because a lot of it has gone away in just a few years. So it's very important that we learn to do something about it.

We can all help to stop the ozone layer from disappearing! For more ideas on how to do that, keep reading!

THANK YOU FOR SHOPPING AT
CFH
(204) 324-9510

4/21/90   12:46 OFF   0% SALE
SAVE THE EARTH! RECYCLE! REUSE
ASK ABOUT OUR NON-TOXIC PRODUCTS

1313	2	6.95 /EA
13M KID'S BOOKS		13.90
346080	2	2.99 /EA
T1003 3PK TENNIS BALLS		5.98
1608	2	.20 /EA N
EVERYDAY CANDY		.40

SUB-TOTAL: 20.28   TAX: 1.61
                         TOTAL: 21.89
CK#003725 ABA#   CK AMT: 21.89

===>> JRNL# A26087   <<===
      CUST # #5

WATER POLLUTION

WATER, WATER

The planet Earth is mostly water. Oceans cover the biggest part of it—and there are lakes, rivers, streams, and even water underground. All life on Earth—from the littlest bug to the biggest whale—depends on this water. It's precious.

But we're not doing a very good job of keeping water clean. In many places, the water has become polluted.

RIVERS AND LAKES

Rivers and lakes are polluted by garbage, or by poisonous chemicals which are dumped right into them.

UNDERGROUND

Underground water can be polluted by gasoline or other harmful liquids that seep into the ground. Some fertilizers and pesticides used on farms or lawns leak down through the dirt, too.

THE SEAS

The ocean, which is a home to so much life, has been used as a place to dump garbage and poisonous chemicals for a long time. It's getting polluted, too.

OUR MISSION

We need to save our water, to keep it clean and healthy so people, plants and animals will always have some to drink. And so fish and other creatures will have a place to live.

To learn more about what you can do to save water—and keep it clean and healthy—turn to *Preserving Our Oceans, Rivers, Lakes, and Streams*.

WHAT KIDS SAY

ABOUT WATER POLLUTION

"If we the people pollute the water, we will kill the fish and the animals that live nearby will die, too. Then it will make the food chain out of order. Then we will die because the food chain is not in order."

—*Joey Leichter, Age 10*

"If people want to live and be healthy, they need to care a hoot about our lakes."

—*Emika Porter, Age 10*

ABOUT AIR POLLUTION

"People shouldn't use cars as much, so that it doesn't pollute the air. If we're not careful, no one will be able to breathe the air and everyone will have to wear gas masks."

—*Regan Horner, Age 10*

"No gases! No air pollution! It's *life* or *death*."

—*Jesse Hornstein, Age 10,*

"Air pollution is devastating. It is the worst thing. I hate the way it makes the air smell."

—*Emika Porter, Age 10*

ABOUT THE OZONE HOLE

"Everyone knows that the ozone layer is very important. Without it we would all be a bunch of sorry people. So we should all stop using things that have chemicals in them that eat the ozone layer. If we do this we can save the ozone layer."

—*Maya Crayton, Age 10*

"I don't know why somebody made CFCs and halons, but I do think it was a dumb idea."

—*David Moser, Age 11*

ABOUT WILDLIFE

"Trees are getting cut down.... But we need the trees. And wild animals need the trees too, to live in."

—*Shannon Lemmons, Age 10*

"We need to help animals so they will not become extinct."

—*Shiquela Smith, Age 10*

ABOUT THE GARBAGE CRUNCH

"We have to stop buying things that we can only use once and then throw away."

—*Karen Leason, Age 10*

"There is too much garbage in the world. The landfills will get so overcrowded that we will be living around garbage every day... If we would recycle more, we wouldn't have such a BAD garbage problem!"

—*Lauren Weber, Age 10*

ABOUT THE GREENHOUSE EFFECT

"I think global warming and the greenhouse effect are very bad! What do we want the earth to become, a flaming ball?"

—*Adam Adler, Age 10*

"Why are we letting the greenhouse effect happen? It doesn't make sense. I think it's time we got together and kept our home the right temperature for living things."

—*Jessamine Catalfo, Age 10*

GUARDING OUR

OUR

BURIED
TREASURES

TREASURE
THOUGHTS

Buried treasure! It makes you think of pirates and hidden chests full of gold.

But gold is only one of the buried treasures in our Earth. There are many wonderful things that this planet has been storing up for billions of years. How many can you name? There's oil, iron, silver, sand, aluminum, copper. . .you could go on and on.

These treasures are a gift to us. We heat our homes with them in the winter, we make them into tools, we cook with them. . .in fact, there's practically nothing that we don't use them for.

But there's a limited amount of them. When we use them all up, there will be *no more*. So it's up to us to decide—what should we do with them? Should we take them all out of the Earth and turn them into things we don't really need? Or should we save them so we—and all the creatures of the Earth—will still have them?

Sounds like a silly question. . .yet, we haven't asked it often enough.

Now it's your turn to ask the question—and come up with the answers. After all, the Earth's buried treasures belong to you, too.

1. BE A BOTTLE BANDIT

Take A Guess.
What is glass made from?
A) Frozen water   B) Sand   C) Venetian blinds

Light bulbs, windows, TVs, mirrors...What do they all have in common? Glass.

Look around. See how much glass we use.

Now here's an amazing thought: We throw most of our glass away.

Every month, we toss out enough glass bottles and jars to fill up a giant skyscraper.

You probably think this doesn't make much sense, since we're just making more garbage, and wasting the Earth's treasures besides. And you're right.

This is especially true because we can reuse all those bottles and jars—we can recycle them!

Did You Know

• Glass is recycled at factories where they break bottles and jars into little bits, then melt them down and mix them with new glass.

• People have been making glass for over 3,000 years. So when Nero was fiddling in ancient Rome, he probably had a bottle of something to drink right next to him.

• For a long time, glass was considered precious. Then people got so good at making it that we started thinking of it as garbage.

Answer: B. That's right, glass is made from heating and molding sand.

- Now we throw out *28 billion* bottles and jars every year!
- Recycling glass saves energy for making new glass. The energy saved from recycling *one* glass bottle will light a 100-watt light bulb for four hours.

What You Can Do

To recycle glass bottles and jars in your home

- Find a place you can keep a box or two for collecting glass.
- If you have enough room, keep a different box for each different color of glass—brown, green, clear. Otherwise, you might have to sort the glass later.
- Take the caps, corks or rings off the bottles and jars. It's okay to leave the paper labels on, but rinse the glass out before you put it in the box.
- Once you've got a place to put the glass, it only takes about 15 minutes a week to keep up the recycling.
- Ask an adult to find out where the nearest recycling center is. Your neighborhood may even have curbside recycling.
- Every week or two, gather the boxes and take them to the recycling center or put them on the curb for pickup.
- Don't forget to pick up bottles wherever you find them, and take them home to recycle.

2. BUY NOW, PLAY LATER

Take A Guess.
How many of your toys were once your mom's or dad's?
A) All of them B) None of them C) Good question

Wow! Did you see that TV commercial about the Super-Amazing Gizmo? It's a transformer that really flies... and it'll do your homework for you, too.

It looks terrific. And, of course, you want one.

But how long will it last?

Think about it. Toys don't just come from toy stores. They come from materials taken out of the Earth. So if they break right away, and you have to buy new ones to replace them, you're not only creating a lot of extra garbage, you're using up the treasures of the Earth.

So what's a kid supposed to do, stop buying toys?

Of course not!

But you can try to buy toys that last.

Did You Know
• Some toys really last. For instance, ancient toys like tops that are over 1,000 years old have been found by explorers.

You can see some of these—and other very old toys—in museums.

• Many people consider old toys family treasures. They are passed down from parent to child to grandchild.

• Imagine playing with a toy that your great-grandfather or grandmother once enjoyed!

Answer: C. Ask about it. Did your parents' toys last? Do they wish they had?

• It takes the same amount of the Earth's "buried treasures" to make a toy that lasts as it does to make one that will break in a few days. But toys that last don't have to be replaced by more toys. That's one way they help save a part of the Earth.

• Another way: Well-made toys don't turn into instant junk. That means they won't get thrown away and fill up the garbage dumps so quickly.

What You Can Do

• When you're in a toy store, and you see something you like, check out how well it's made. Is it cheap plastic that will break and get tossed out right away? Or is it made to last?

• If you're not sure which it is, ask someone—a parent, or a person who works in the store. Tell them you care because it helps the Earth.

• Take care of the toys you already have. Even if a toy is made to last, it needs your help. The better care it gets, the longer it will be around for you—and maybe even your children—to enjoy.

See For Yourself

Go to a toy store (you probably don't need to be told *that* twice). Pick an aisle, and slowly walk along so you can see all the toys for sale. See if you can tell the difference between well-made toys and the kind that will break before long. Which are there more of? What are they made of?

3. DON'T CAN IT!

Take A Guess.
How many times can one aluminum can be recycled?
A) Never B) Just once C) Again and again and again

Before a soda can gets to the store...before it has soda in it...before it's even a can, it is part of the earth!

Soda cans are made of a metal called aluminum. It is very important to us.

We need aluminum for airplanes, cars, bicycles, and many household items—not just for soda cans.

There's still aluminum in the ground, but it won't be a buried treasure forever if we keep digging it up. That's why we have to save it whenever we can, instead of throwing it out.

The best way to preserve it is by recycling—using it over and over again.

Did You Know

• We use over 65 billion aluminum soda cans every year! And we could recycle every one of them!

• Here's how aluminum is recycled: Soda cans and other aluminum products like cat food cans and aluminum foil are col-

lected and sent to factories, where they're ground into little metal chips. Then they're melted down and turned into solid aluminum bars.

Answer: C. Aluminum cans can be recycled over and over and over and over and over...

• The bars are rolled into sheets of aluminum, which are then sold to can makers...who make new cans out of them.

• There is no limit to the number of times aluminum can be melted down and reused. It's amazing! The can you're drinking soda out of today might actually have been part of someone else's soda can 20 years ago!

• Recycling saves energy as well as aluminum. For example: the energy you save from recycling just one aluminum can could keep your TV running for three hours!

What You Can Do

• Recycle aluminum the same way you recycle glass.

• Wash out the cans (it keeps the ants away), then toss them in a box until recycling day.

• Don't forget that clean aluminum foil, pie plates and frozen food trays can be recycled, too.

• Pick up aluminum cans you find on the road, on the ground or anywhere someone has left them. Take them home and recycle.

See For Yourself

• Go to the store and find the aisle with the soda and beer cans in it.

• Count out 250 six-packs. That's quite a lot—in fact, it's 1,500 cans; there may not even be that many in the store. But if there are, it will take you a while to count them all.

• When you're done, take a look at all the cans you've counted. That's how many the average person in this country uses every single year!

• Imagine throwing all of the cans out. What a waste. Now imagine saving them all and using them again. Much better.

4. PRECYCLE IT!

Take A Guess.

Over half of the plastic we buy and throw away each year is just packaging. What happens to it when it's thrown away?
A) Nothing—it just sits there and clutters up the Earth
B) It gets up and starts dancing   C) It watches TV

Did you ever stop to think that when you buy something packaged in plastic or cardboard, you're actually buying and paying for the thing *plus garbage*?

It sounds ridiculous, doesn't it? But that's what happens. You tear off the packaging and stuff it right in the garbage!

If it's plastic packaging, it's made from one of the Earth's greatest buried treasures—oil. It's been underground for millions of years! ... And it may have even been part of a dinosaur once! Think about that!

If we turn oil into plastic, we can never change it back; it can never be part of the Earth again.

So whenever you buy a toy, some food, or anything...you have a terrific chance to help the Earth! Look around. See how things are packaged. Make careful choices. You can do it!

Answer: A. Plastic will be sitting around for hundreds of years, at least! What a mess!

Did You Know

• Each American throws away about 60 pounds of plastic packaging every year! Think about how much *you* weigh. Now think about how much 60 pounds is. That's a lot of plastic.

• Americans use *2.5 million* plastic bottles every *hour*. Can you believe it? And most of them get thrown away.

• Remember when we talked about how our garbage dumps are filling up? Well, about 1/3 of all that garbage is packaging. Less packaging means less garbage.

What You Can Do

• Look for ways to practice *precycling*. That means buying things which come in packages that can be recycled (not turned into garbage), or are made of materials that have *already* been recycled.

• For example: If you go food shopping with your family, buy eggs in cardboard, not Styrofoam, cartons. (Then reuse the cartons for art projects.)

• Some cereal, crackers and cookies come in boxes made of recycled cardboard. It's easy to spot them: recycled cardboard is gray on the inside.

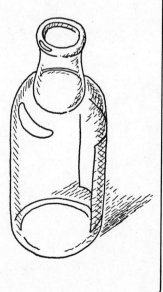

• Many toymakers use expensive packaging to make their toys seem better than they are. Sometimes there's more to the package than to the toy itself! Check it out.

See For Yourself

• Keep a big bag or box handy to collect the packaging you throw away. You'll be surprised at how much you collect in a few days.

5. PASS IT ON

Take A Guess.
How much of the stuff we throw out could be recycled?
A) None of it—garbage is no good for anything
B) Just a little bit   C) Half of it

Wouldn't it be great if there was a way to help save the Earth, get rid of stuff you don't want and make someone happy, all at the same time?

There is.

Instead of throwing away your old things, you can find a new home for them

You know those old board games you don't play with anymore...or that Dr. Seuss book you've outgrown...or those easy puzzles you can do with your eyes closed? Try passing them on rather than tossing them out.

You'll be saving a little piece of our Earth. And someone else might love them.

Did You Know

• Since the things you use are all made from materials that come from the Earth, they're still valuable, even when you don't need them anymore.

• By passing them on to other people instead of throwing

Answer: C. That's enough garbage to fill a football stadium from top to bottom every day!

them away, you can make less garbage and save precious resources.

• Some groups, like the Salvation Army, collect used things to sell in stores.

• Used books are often collected by libraries for special book sales that raise money to buy new library books.

• Old games and toys can often be donated to hospitals or other places where kids need something to play with.

What You Can Do

• Go through your closet, your attic, your basement...even look under your bed! Find the things you don't want any more, but which someone else might love.

• Find places that can use your old things. Look in the phone book and write down the numbers for your local hospital, library, Salvation Army, and so on. Call them.

• Have a garage sale. A boy we know keeps all his old things in a closet. Once a year, he puts up signs in his neighborhood that say "Garage Sale at 33 Edgewood St., 9 AM to 5 PM on

Saturday." Then he puts all his things out on the driveway or lawn, and puts a price on each of them. People come and buy what they want. Then he gives the rest of it away. It's a great way to make money and recycle at the same time.

6. COLORS
OF THE EARTH

Take A Guess.
What can you make with an old egg carton?
A) A million dollars B) An art project C) Supper

There are some places in the world where kids don't have markers or crayons or store-bought paints. But they still get to draw and paint and make beautiful art.

What do they do? They make colorful inks and stains from the juices of plants, vegetables, or fruits.

Of course, we're not suggesting that you go squeeze a strawberry the next time you want to make something red (though it might be fun!).

But there are other ways to keep the Earth in mind when you color, draw, or paint.

Did You Know

• Most crayons are made from oil. Since oil comes from prehistoric creatures, you might be coloring with the last remains of a Tyrannosaurus Rex!

• Have you ever made pictures with markers? Some have chemicals with names like "toluene" and "ethanol" in them.

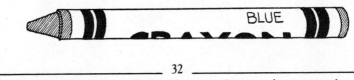

BLUE

Answer: B. Egg cartons and other "throwaways" are great for art projects!

Creating these chemicals makes pollution and uses oil. And the fumes they give off can be bad for you.

• Glue sticks, rubber cement, and glue sometimes have the same types of pollution-causing chemicals in them.

What You Can Do

• Use beeswax crayons. They aren't made from oil.

• Use water-based paints. If you're not sure whether your paint is water-based, ask a parent or other adult.

• Paint and draw on recycled paper.

• Use water-based markers and glue.

• When you use art supplies, remember that they're made with the Earth's treasures. Have fun with them, and try your best not to waste them.

See For Yourself

What's the most creative way to recycle? Make up your own art projects. You can use almost anything—from old egg cartons, to pieces of fabric, to plastic. Art projects from recycled materials look good and are lots of fun to do. Try a collage or a mobile made from recycled things you save during the week.

• If you'd like to get some beeswax crayons, but can't find any in your area, you can order them by mail from Seventh Generation, 10 Farrell St., South Burlington, VT 05403.

7. STAMP OUT STYROFOAM

Take A Guess.
If you lined up all the Styrofoam cups made in
just one day, how far would they reach?
A) A mile B) Around the Earth C) Across the U.S.

Y ou may not know the word "Styrofoam," but you know the stuff. It's a kind of material we use for things like

throwaway cups, packing things in boxes, and for keeping "food to go" warm. Lots of fast-food restaurants serve their hamburgers in Styrofoam packages.

Styrofoam is a kind of plastic, so making it uses up treasures that have been on the Earth for billions of years.

And what do we do with it? Go take a look in a fast-food garbage can. Does that styro-trash look like the Earth's treasures to you? Not anymore!

Using Styrofoam means using up precious resources. . .and adding more garbage to our world. Is that what you want? Or do you—and your planet—deserve something better?

Did You Know

• Styrofoam is permanent garbage. It can't *ever* become part of the Earth again. Five hundred years from now a boy might be digging in his backyard and find a piece of the Styrofoam cup you drank lemonade from on a picnic last week!

Answer: B. Incredible! They would circle the entire planet ... and reach a little further, too!

• Styrofoam is a danger to sea animals. Floating in the water, it looks like their food. But when they eat it, they're in trouble. Sea turtles, for example, sometimes eat Styrofoam and then—because it makes them float—can't dive again. It eventually clogs their systems, and then they starve to death.

What You Can Do

• Avoid Styrofoam. Such plastic foam is often made with chemicals that make the ozone hole bigger!

• If you eat at fast-food restaurants, ask for paper cups and plates. If the people at the restaurant say they don't have them, explain why you don't want to use Styrofoam. Tell them that, as much as you like their food, you really don't want to do anything to hurt the Earth.

• Try to avoid Styrofoam products like picnic plates, cups, and even (if you ever go food shopping) egg cartons.

8. FEED THE WORMS

Take A Guess.
Which of these is something a worm won't eat?
A) A juicy steak B) Dirt C) Vegetables

When you're done with your dinner, is there still a little food left on your plate? What are you going to do with it? This may sound strange, but you don't have to throw it away. You can save it, and turn it back into rich, fertile soil—one of the Earth's greatest treasures. Then you can use it for growing plants.

This is called composting. It's so simple that anyone can do it.

Did You Know

• You can make compost with leaves and grass clippings, or food scraps. Any garbage that's *organic*—which means "made out of things that were once alive"—will work.

• Boy, do we have plenty of *organic* garbage to use! More than half of the trash your family throws away every year is organic.

• In fact, every year each of us tosses out about 1,200 pounds of organic garbage!

• How much is that? Well, if you weigh 100 lbs., then the organic garbage you throw away in a year weighs about twelve times as much as you do!

Answer: A. Worms don't eat meat.

• If we composted that garbage instead of throwing it away, we wouldn't have such a big trash problem.

What You Can Do

There are many easy ways to compost.

• By yourself: The simplest way is to make a pile of leaves and grass clippings in a corner of your yard. In a while, the pile will turn into soil.

• With an adult: build a special bin for compost and put all your organic garbage in it. Turn it over every once in a while, and watch it slowly become a part of the Earth again.

• The most interesting way to compost is with worms. Worms? Believe it or not, they're great composters. With your parents or teacher, build a wooden box about two feet wide, two feet long, and eight inches deep. Fill the box with moist bedding, like peat moss. Then buy some red worms at a local nursery (or maybe a bait shop) and put them in. You can put in household garbage that isn't meat or bones, or a fatty food. Mix them into the box, and then stand back! The worms will eat the rotting garbage and actually make soil—some of the richest, most fertile soil around.

See For Yourself

For more information on composting, write to the Seattle Tilth Association, 2649 Sunnyvale Ave. N., Seattle, WA 98103. For $2.50 and a self-addressed envelope with $.50 return postage on it, you can get their helpful brochure, *Home Composting*.

9. USE IT AGAIN...AND AGAIN...AND AGAIN...

Take A Guess.
How many disposable plastic bottles do we use in four days?
A) Enough to fill a truck B) Enough to fill a warehouse
C) As many as there are people in the whole U.S.

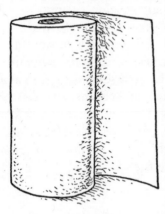

Long before you were born, back when your grandparents were kids, there was no such thing as a paper towel or a paper napkin. People used cloth. Back then, everything was used again and again. In fact, most people would never have imagined throwing something away after using it just once.

But today, we have lots of things that are made especially to be tossed in the garbage after one use; we call them "disposable." Aluminum foil, plastic bags, paper bags, plastic food wrap, and other products are all considered "disposable."

What's going on? Our Earth's treasures are being thrown out as trash. Wouldn't it be wonderful if everyone did a little something to stop this waste? Just imagine what a difference it would make!

Did You Know
• We use millions of feet of paper towels every year. That's a lot of trees!
• Americans use 35 million paper clips every day.
• Americans buy 500 million disposable lighters every year. That's millions of pounds of plastic made by factories just so grown-ups can throw it away.

Answer: C. 240 million! Incredible!

What You Can Do

• Keep a cloth towel by the sink. Next time you rinse your hands or need to wipe up a spill, grab the cloth towel instead of a paper one.

• Keep a "rag bag" handy. Put your old, torn clothes in it, and you'll have a supply of rags to help you out with messy chores or art projects.

• Save plastic bags—you can use them again. If they're dirty, turn them inside out, rinse them and hang them up to dry.

• Aluminum foil is reusable. Wash it off, let it dry, and put it away. When it can't be used again, recycle it.

• Have you got some reusable food containers in your kitchen? (You know, the kind with snap-on tops.) Use them instead of just covering or wrapping food with plastic wrap.

• Start an Earth-positive lunchtime trend—use a lunchbox to carry your food to school. Or if you take a bag lunch, bring home the paper and plastic bags so you can reuse them.

See For Yourself

Look around your house for some "disposable" things. Try to picture where they come from. Hold up a roll of paper towels and imagine it's a tree. Take a plastic bag or plastic wrap and try to see it as oil—or even better, a prehistoric creature. See aluminum foil as a precious metal from underground. They seem a lot more important now, don't they? They are!

PRESERVING OUR OCEANS,

RIVERS, LAKES AND STREAMS

WATER THOUGHTS

Each year there are more and more people living on the Earth, yet the amount of water we have to use remains the same. When we turn on the faucet, fresh water flows out from the same reserves in the ground, from the same rivers and streams.

If you imagine a day without water, you realize how precious it is. But with a little care, you can use water without wasting it.

Do you know what you do affects our streams, lakes, rivers, and oceans? No matter where you live, your actions influence what happens to them—and what happens to the animals that depend on them.

Think of all the ways that people have used our oceans and waterways for food, transportation, trash disposal, energy and recreation. Because the oceans have seemed so vast and our water supplies have seemed to abundant, we haven't been careful. Now we need to change the way we think and act. We need to repair the damage that has been done.

Fortunately, all of us can help to protect our lakes, streams, rivers and oceans. By being a leak detective, a water-saver, and a beach buddy, you can make a difference. And you can have fun doing it.

—Marydele Donnelly,
Center for Marine Conservation

10. BE A WATER-LEAK DETECTIVE

Take A Guess.
If a leaky faucet fills a coffee cup in 10 minutes, how much water will it waste in a year? Enough for:
A) A glass of water B)A bath C) 52 baths

Calling all kids! Calling all kids! Be on the lookout for hidden water leaks in your house. Secret hiding places include: behind the walls, in faucets, in toilets…and even outside at the end of a hose.

Your mission as a water-leak detective is to find the hidden leaks…and help to stop them!

Did You Know

• Even a tiny leak can waste a lot of water. For example, a leak that fills up a coffee cup in 10 minutes will waste over 3,000 gallons of water in a year.

• How much water is that? You'd have to drink 65 glasses of water every day *for a year* to get that much water!

• 20% of all the toilets in American homes are leaking right now.…And usually people don't even know it.

• In one year, a leaky toilet can waste over 22,000 gallons of water. That's enough to take three baths every day!

42

What You Can Do

Be a Water-Leak Detective. Here's how:

• First, get your parent to teach you how to read the water meter. If you have one, it will probably be in the corner of your basement, on the outside wall of your house, or next to the street, under a cement or metal cover.

• Then pick a time when everyone is going to be out of the house, and no one will be using the water—when the whole family is about to go out shopping or to a movie, for example.

• Before you leave, read the water meter and write down its setting. Then when you get back home, take another reading. If the numbers have changed, you've probably discovered a leak! Tell your parents what you've found.

Another way to be a leak detective: Check your toilet.

• Get an adult to take the top off the toilet tank in your home. Then put about 12 drops of red or blue food coloring in the tank.

• Wait about 15 minutes. Guard the toilet, so no one uses it while you're waiting. That's important.

• Now look in the toilet. If colored water shows up in the bowl, you've found a leak!

11. PRESTO, ON!... PRESTO, OFF!

Take A Guess.
You can save 20,000 gallons of water a year by not letting the water run. That's enough to fill:
A) A garbage can B)A big truck C)A swimming pool

Imagine pumping water or hauling it from a well every time you wanted to brush your teeth, like they used to in the old days. It was hard work!

Life is easier now. We can just turn on a faucet and...presto...water! In fact, it's so easy to get water that we let *gallons* of it go down the drain without thinking!

We need a little water-saving magic: Presto, on!...and Presto, off! Don't go with the flow!

Did You Know

• Water comes out of the faucet faster than you think. For example: While you're waiting for water to get cold enough to have a drink, you could fill *six* half-gallon milk cartons!

• If you leave the water running while you brush your teeth, you can waste five gallons of water. That's enough to fill 13 cans of soda!

• If you leave the water running while you wash the dishes, you can waste 30 gallons of water—enough to wash a whole car!

44

What You Can Do

• When you brush your teeth: Just wet your brush, then turn off the water…and then turn it on again when you need to rinse your brush off. You'll save up to nine gallons of water each time! That's enough to give your pet a bath.

• When you wash dishes: If you just fill up the basin and rinse dishes in it, instead of letting the water run, you can save up to 25 gallons each time. That's enough to take a five-minute shower.

• When you're going to take a bath: Plug the tub before you let the water run, so you don't waste any.

• When you're thirsty: If you like cool water, why not leave a bottle of it in the refrigerator instead of letting the water run? You'll save water, and still have a cool drink.

See For Yourself

• How long do you think it will take to fill a milk carton with water? To find out, get an empty half-gallon milk carton and a grown-up with a watch to time you.

• Open the milk carton and hold it under the faucet.

• Turn on the faucet and time it.

• How long did it take to fill the carton? Imagine that all over the U.S., people are letting the water run like that. Don't be one of them! P.S. Don't waste that water by pouring it down the sink—pour it on a thirsty plant instead. Good work.

12. SEE YOU AT THE BEACH!

Take A Guess.
What are you most likely to find on a beach?
A) Monsters   B) Sand castles   C) Lots of garbage

Flash! Warning! Flash! Warning! We need help! Our beaches are in trouble. There's garbage in the ocean. There's litter on the beach.

This is serious. Lots of animals live in the ocean. And we can't live without oceans, either. We get most of our air, moisture, and even weather from them.

But what can one kid do? You can't save the whole ocean by yourself....But you can help to save a little piece of it. Here are some things to think about, next time you go to the beach.

Did You Know
• Plastic bags and other plastic garbage thrown into the ocean kill as many as a million sea creatures every year!

• Most of this is thrown from boats. But some of it comes from beaches or overflowing garbage cans nearby.

• Plastic floating in the sea often looks like food to ocean animals. For example: plastic bags look like jellyfish to sea turtles, which swallow them and then die.

Answer: C. Unfortunately, people forget that animals live on the beach, too.

- Birds also get in trouble. They sometimes mistake little bits of plastic for food and choke on them.
- So you might save an animal's life just by picking up plastic from a beach.

What You Can Do

- Don't throw any kind of litter on the beach.
- When you visit the beach, take along a large garbage bag. Try to fill it with trash, close it tight, then throw it in a garbage can. (If there are none on the beach, take the bag with you.)
- If you find any bottles or aluminum cans on the beach, bring them home for recycling.
- If you go fishing, never, never throw fishing line in the water. Birds and sea creatures can get tangled in it and die.

See For Yourself

- Every year, there's a big beach cleanup all over the world. People get together and patrol beaches in their area for three hours. They pick up millions of pounds of garbage and save many animals.
- Does that sound like fun? Write and find out more about it. Send a letter to: The Center for Marine Conservation, 1725 DeSales Street NW, Suite 500, Washington, D.C. 20036. They'll send you information.

13. TOILET TALK

Take A Guess.
Where do you use most of the drinkable water in your house?
A) The kitchen sink B) The garden hose C) The toilet

Toilets?!! It may seem kind of funny to be talking about toilets when we're supposed to be talking about saving the Earth. But there is a connection. We use more water in our toilets than in any other place in our homes.

But a lot of it is wasted, because most toilets use more water than they need to.

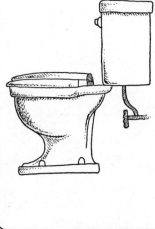

Here's something simple you can do to help turn your toilet into a water-saver.

Did You Know

• Believe it or not, the water we flush down our toilets starts out as fresh drinking water!

• Fresh water flows into the tank (in the back of the toilet). When

Answer: C. The toilet. You may not think of it as drinkable water, but it is, before you use it.

you push the handle to flush, the water flows through the bowl to clean it out and goes down into the sewer. Then the tank fills up with more fresh water.

• Each time you flush, your toilet uses about five to seven gallons of water! But it doesn't have to!

What You Can Do

• Here's a fun project The object is to put something in your toilet tank to take up space, so there will be less room, and your toilet will use less water.

• The best thing to put in the tank is a plastic jug, like the kind you get laundry soap, milk, or juice in.

• First, soak off the label.

• Then get some small rocks and put them in the jug to make it heavier. Fill it with water and put the cap back on. You might need help carrying the jug, now because it can get heavy.

• Now get an adult to lift the toilet tank cover off.

• Put the bottle in the tank. Be careful that it doesn't get in the way of the arm or chain that helps the toilet to flush.

• Now every time you flush, you'll save between one and two gallons of water. Good for you!

See For Yourself

Discover how the toilet works. Ask one of your parents to take off the top of the toilet tank. Then flush the toilet. Watch as the arm inside lifts and the water flows from the tank into the bowl, then swirls away into the drain. Now watch while the tank fills up with water again, so it's ready the next time you need to flush. What a clever invention!

14. SHOWER POWER

Take A Guess.
How many milk cartons can you fill with the water from a five-minute shower?
A) 5   B) 15   C) 50

What if you turned on the faucet and no water came out? We need to save water now so that will never happen!

One thing you can do is check to see if your shower is using too much water. There's an easy test you can do to find out. It's on the next page.

Did You Know
• When you shower, you use five gallons of water *every minute!* How much is that? Enough to fill 40 big glasses!

• A whole shower usually takes at least five minutes. So every day, you could use *25 gallons* of water taking one shower.

• In a year, that's almost 10,000 gallons for your showers!

• Taking a bath uses even more water than showers—about twice as much. A bath can easily use 50 gallons of water.

• Shower Secret: People can put in a special "low-flow" shower head. This adds air to the water, so it cuts the amount of shower water used from five gallons a minute to two-and-a-half. That's half as much water! But it feels great!

What You Can Do
• Take showers instead of baths. This saves water right away. One bonus: singing in a shower sounds better than in a bath.

Answer: C. Think how high 50 milk cartons stacked on top of one another would reach!

• Tell your parents about "low-flow" shower heads. Believe it or not, most grown-ups have never heard of them. You could even phone the hardware store to help find one. Or write a letter to Ecological Water Products, 1341 West Main Rd., Middletown, RI 02840 and ask for information. (If you do this, don't forget to show it to your parents.)

See For Yourself

The World Famous Shower Head Milk Carton Test.

Are you using too much water in your shower? Take this test to find out.

• You need an empty milk carton, a watch with a second hand, and an adult to time you.

• Open up the top of the milk carton so it forms a square.

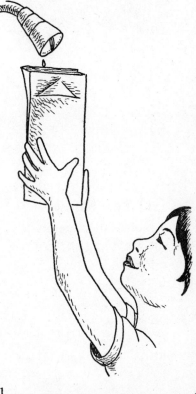

• Turn on the water so it's a normal shower flow. Then get in (not with all your clothes on, of course) and hold the milk carton up to the shower head for 10 seconds. The adult with the watch should tell you when to start, and when the time is up.

• If the carton overflows in less than 10 seconds, your shower head uses too much water.

15. DON'T DUMP IT!

Take A Guess.
Which of these would you want in your drinking water?
A) Furniture polish B) Paint thinner C) Motor oil

If you dug a hole as far as you could go, would you ever reach China? Of course not. But you *would* reach water! Underground, there's lots of fresh water. We need to take care of it, to keep it clean for all living things. How can you take care of something underground? Simple—just make sure nothing harmful is spilled on the ground that will soak down into our water!

Did You Know
• Most of the water in the world isn't drinkable!

• The oceans cover 2/3 of the Earth, but ocean water is salty, so no one can drink it.

52

Answer: None, of course. But if we don't dispose of them properly, they end up in our water!

- There's a lot of water in the polar ice caps, but we can't drink ice. And we can't just melt a part of the world.
- So what's left for us? The water in lakes, rivers, streams …and what's underground. That's called *groundwater*.
- Where does *your* water come from? Do you know? More than half the people in America get theirs from groundwater. In fact, 90% of all the water on Earth that human beings can drink right now is underground.
- It's really easy to pollute groundwater. Just dumping common, everyday things on the ground can do it because the Earth is like a sponge that soaks everything in.
- For example, a gallon of paint or a quart of motor oil can seep into the Earth and pollute 250,000 gallons of drinking water. And a spilled gallon of gasoline can pollute 750,000 gallons of water! The poison (called *insecticide*) that farmers and gardeners put out to kill bugs also can soak into the ground and pollute our water.

What You Can Do

- Be careful about what you spill on the Earth. You can't avoid some accidents, but don't dump harmful liquids onto the ground on purpose.
- When you're not sure what to do with a can of oil, or paint or gasoline, bring it to an adult. Ask the adult to make sure the lid is on tight, and the can should be stored where smaller kids can't get to it. But the can shouldn't be thrown in the garbage! It should be saved for a special garbage pick-up called "toxic waste collection."
- You probably won't be using much paint, motor oil or gasoline soon…but it's not too early to think about this.

16. THE LAWN RANGER

Take A Guess.
What's the best way to sweep a driveway or patio clean?
A)A regular broom   B) A water hose   C)An electric fan

D o you water the lawn at your house? A lot of kids get that job during the summer. If you're one of them, here are some water-saving tips for you.

Did You Know
• In the summertime, Americans use about 1/3 more water than they do the rest of the year. Why? Because we're watering our lawns.

• There are 20 million acres of lawns in the U.S. To water that much grass, we need 540 billion gallons of water every single week! That's enough to give every person in the world a shower for four days in a row!

• Some people think that the more you water your lawn, the better it is. But that's not true. Most lawns are watered twice as much as they need to be. This means that with the water many people now use on their lawns, they could actually water two lawns. What a huge waste of water!

• Actually, most lawns only need an inch of water each week.

What You Can Do
• Water only early in the morning or in the evening, when the chances of the water drying up in the heat—that's called *evaporation*—are the lowest.

• Don't water on windy days. The wind just blows the water

Answer: A. A broom! But too many people use a hose and waste lots of precious water.

away.

• Make sure your sprinklers are watering the lawn and not the sidewalk or driveway—they never grow anything!

• Use a watering can or hose for small areas that need more water. Be sure to water slowly and deeply, so the roots that need the water the most are able to get it.

See For Yourself

There's a simple test—we call it the "inch test"—which you can do to find out how long your sprinkler should be on. You'll need a ruler, a watch and three cans.

• Set the cans on your lawn. One should be close to the sprinkler; one should be medium distance away; and the last should be at the far end of the sprinkler's reach.

• Now turn on the sprinkler. Check every few minutes and see how long it takes for an inch of water to build up in each can. Write down how long it takes for each one.

• Add the three times together and divide by three to get an *average* time. (You may need an older sister or brother, or adult, to help with the math.)

• The number you get is the amount of time you need to water your lawn for it to get an inch of water. If you water the lawn that long each week, it will get the water it needs, but not too much.

• Check it out: Call up the company that supplies water for your area, and ask them if an inch a week is the right amount where you live.

17. ADOPT A STREAM

Take A Guess.
Which of these would you probably find in a stream?
A) Fish   B) Old tires   C) Pebbles

Streams and creeks are great places to play. They're fun to explore, wade in, skip rocks in....They're even fun to listen to. And if you stay very quiet awhile, you may see some birds or other animals—because they depend on streams, too.

Unfortunately, lots of streams have become polluted or filled with garbage. Someone needs to help make them clean again. How about it? You and your friends can help take care of the Earth by adopting a stream in your area.

Did You Know

• The color and smell of a stream can tell you a lot about what's happening to it.

• **Green water:** Can mean very small plants called algae are in the water. This makes it hard for any other life to exist in the stream.

• **Muddy water:** Can mean there's too much dirt in the water, which makes it hard for fish to breathe. The stream may need more plants along its bank.

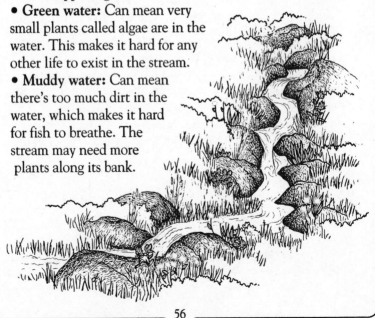

Answer: You'd find all of them. Fish and pebbles belong in streams, but old tires don't!

- **A shiny film on the water:** Can mean there's oil leaking into the stream. That's poison and should be stopped.
- **Foam or suds in the water:** Can mean soap from homes or factories is leaking in.
- **Rotten egg smell:** Bad news! Sewage could be leaking into the stream! Sewage carries germs that can make us very sick, and kill water life.
- **Orange or red coating on the water:** Might mean a factory is dumping pollutants into the stream.
- If you find fish, or lots of bugs, in the water, that's a good sign. It means there's lots of oxygen there.

What You Can Do

- Patrol the stream bank and pick up all the trash you can find. Make sure you put the trash in a trash can, or bring a garbage bag with you and take it back to your house to throw away.

- Try not to let your pet leave its waste in or near a stream. Animal waste can pollute the water in a stream.

- Organize a party to plant trees along stream banks. This will keep the soil from washing away into the stream and protect animals that live in the stream as well.

- If you find anything like oil or sewage leaking into the water, report it to a parent or other adult.

See For Yourself

Send for their free Save Our Streams booklet and other information, write to:
The Izaak Walton League of America
1401 Wilson Blvd., Level B
Arlington, VA 22209

PROTECTING

ANIMALS

WILD THOUGHTS

Why should we bother taking care of animals?

You probably wouldn't really ask such a silly question. Kids understand why animals are important better than grown-ups do.

But it's still a good question to think about.

Here's one reason: Every creature on the Earth deserves to have a good life. And sometimes we can help.

Here's another reason: Every animal is part of the beautiful chain of nature that exists on our Earth. The littlest insect is as important to the survival of all life on the planet as the biggest elephant or the smartest person. All of us have a special place in the world.

What happens if one kind of animal disappears? Maybe nothing we can notice. . .but something changes on our Earth.

It makes sense to protect all animals. And it feels good. And on top of that, it's fun.

So that answers the question, doesn't it?

18. FOR THE BIRDS

Take A Guess.
What is a hummingbird's favorite food?
A) Hot oatmeal B) Sweet syrup C) Corn-on-the-cob

S plash! Ruffle! Splash! Have you ever watched a bird take a bath? It dips in, fluffs itself up, shakes all over, flaps its wings and dips and flaps some more....And it looks like it's having the greatest time. Probably it is!

That's why there are so many birds in yards with birdbaths. Setting up a bath or feeder is a great way to bring birds into your yard.

And when you do, you not only get to enjoy the birds, you also get to help the Earth.

Did You Know

• Birds are always hungry! They use up so much energy that they need to eat all the time.

• Sometimes birds eat 4/5 of their own weight in one day!

• What does that mean? Let's say you weigh 100 pounds. If you were a bird, you would have to eat 80 pounds of food between the time you woke up in the morning and the time you went to sleep at night! You can't do it! But birds can.

• Birds need water to drink (especially in summer) and to keep clean. They can have anywhere from 940 to 25,000 feathers, so they've got a lot of washing to do!

What You Can Do

• Make a birdfeeder for peanuts! Take a bunch of unsalted peanuts still in their shells, and tie them on a piece of yarn or string. Hang the string from a branch; birds will find it.

• Another nutty idea: Spread peanut butter all over a pine cone. Be sure to fill up all the little spaces. Then hang the pine cone outside. Lots of birds like peanut butter.

• Hang some orange peels from trees—a great bird snack!

Make a Birdbath

• Find a big ceramic or plastic saucer like the kind under potted plants. (Don't use metal—it will get too hot in the summer and freeze in the winter.) It should have some kind of edge around it for birds to rest on.

• Birds don't need the water to be too deep—about two inches is perfect. Keep the bath filled with water.

• If there are cats in the neighborhood, you might need to put the birdbath up high or hang it from a tree.

See For Yourself

For more information on bird feeding and birdbaths, write to The National Audubon Society, 645 Pennsylvania Ave. SE, Washington, D.C. 20003

19. IN YOUR OWN BACKYARD

Take A Guess.
What will a red currant bush attract to your backyard?
A) Space creatures B) Butterflies C) Grizzly bears

Where do wild animals live?
In the jungle? Yes.
In the forest? Uh-huh.
In the desert? You bet.

But guess what—they also live in cities, in suburbs, in backyards.

Wild animals? Yes!

Squirrels, birds, butterflies, and lots of other creatures live right near people. They're all a part of the wild and wonderful Earth. And you can help them.

Did You Know

• Planting flowers, trees or shrubs is a great way to give animals food and shelter in your own backyard.

• For example: You can attract butterflies with brightly colored flowers.

• Hummingbirds love red flowers.

Answer: B. You can create a home for animals just by planting the right bush or plant.

- Bats and moths like sweet-smelling white flowers.
- Some flowers, called *annuals*, are great for attracting birds. Why? Because they have lots of seeds....And you know how birds love seeds! Sunflowers, zinnias and asters are *annuals*.

What You Can Do

- Design and plant a garden—or a windowsill—full of flowers that will attract animals to your backyard.
- Start a brush pile (bushes, branches, etc.) for small animals to use as "cover." If animals know they can hide themselves when they need to, they're more likely to visit you.
- Contact a nursery or garden center near you to find out what kinds of plants will provide food and good cover for the wildlife you want as "neighbors."

See For Yourself

- The National Wildlife Federation has a Wildlife Habitat Program which will help you create a wild backyard. They'll send you information and a list of helpful books. Study the info and come up with an idea of what you want to do.
- You can send your backyard plan and $5 to them; they'll look it over, make recommendations, and certify your yard as an official Backyard Wildlife Habitat.
- Write to:

National Wildlife Federation
Backyard Wildlife
Habitat Program, 1412 16th
Street NW, Washington,
D.C. 20036.

20. DON'T GET BUGGED

Take A Guess.
Which are there more of on the Earth?
A)People   B)Ants   C)Dogs

Bugs! Ugh! What good are they? You'd be surprised!

Bugs are an important part of keeping the Earth healthy. In fact, we couldn't live without them!

Really? Really!

Did You Know

• Worms may be gross, but believe it or not, we wouldn't be able to grow food without them. Why? Because they eat their way through dirt and leave behind rich soil that plants love.

• In an area about the size of a football field, you could find close to *two million* worms!

• Bees are necessary, too. As they travel from flower to flower gathering pollen to make honey (they make 60,000 trips to flowers just to make one teaspoon of honey!), they spread pollen to other plants as well. The plants can then make seeds, which means more of them will grow. Since we need plants to stay alive, we owe the bees a lot!

• There are more than 2,000 different kinds of spiders in

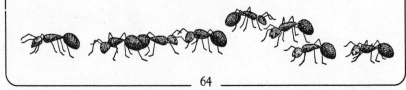

Answer: B. There are more ants than people or dogs, even more than both added together!

America. Sure, they're scary, but they really make our lives better. Why? Because they eat other bugs like mosquitoes and flies. Without spiders, we'd be overrun with bugs. In fact, scientists guess that the bugs spiders eat in *one year* weigh as much as all the people on the Earth! That's heavy!

What You Can Do

• Next time you see a bug on a sidewalk, help it out. Gently pick it up and move it out of the way, where no one will step on it. You've just saved a life!

• If you find a bug in your house, help it to get outside—or leave it alone and let it find its own way out. This might mean opening a window to let it fly out, or picking it up on a piece of paper and taking it outside yourself. The bug probably never meant to visit you, and wandered into your house by accident. Note: If it's a stinging bug, ask for an adult's help in moving it.

• Adopt a spider. Watch it. Admire it. Get grossed out by it. But don't kill it. When you see a spider spin its web, catch a fly and even—ugh!—eat it, you're watching a real-life adventure that's even better than TV!

See For Yourself

The next time you eat an apple, take the core outside and put it in the corner of the yard. Every day, take a look. You'll probably see bugs on the core, eating it or carrying little pieces away. They're helping to break it down and get rid of it. They're cleaning up and recycling, doing their part to keep order in nature and protect the Earth.

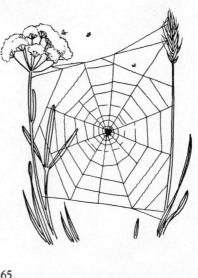

21. SPEND WISELY

Take A Guess.
Why have half of the African elephants disappeared in ten years?
A)They died from old age   B) They left for a warmer place
C)They were killed by people for the ivory in their tusks

I t's hard to imagine that a trip to a supermarket could
help save a wild anmal in Africa, or a dolphin swimming
free in the ocean. But it can. Everything we do—even
shopping—is connected to the rest of the world.

Did You Know

• Things are often brought to American stores from places
like Africa or South America, because people in our country
want to buy them.

• Sometimes this affects animals in a terrible way. For example: Because shoppers wanted to buy ivory, hunters killed

hundreds
of thou-
sands of
elephants
—so many,
in fact,
that ex-
perts are
worried
they might
become
extinct!
This awful
tragedy
happened
just be-
cause peo-
ple were

Answer: C. So sad, but true!

willing to pay for something that came from an animal.

• Right now there's a problem involving dolphins. Dolphins are among the most intelligent animals on Earth, with large brains and an amazing ability to communicate—even with people! They are wonderful creatures.

• For some reason, dolphins like to swim near yellowfin tuna in the ocean. So when some tuna fishermen put out their huge nets, they also catch dolphins. In recent years, more than 6.5 million dolphins have been killed in nets!

• The problem is that the fishermen use nets that catch everything in their path, even things they don't want. When these fishermen catch dolphins, for example, they just kill them or let them die. They don't have any use for them.

What You Can Do

• Don't buy anything made out of ivory, tortoise shell, coral, reptile skins, or cat pelts. All of these things come from endangered animals or plants.

• Learn about endangered species in your very own neighborhood. Visit a local park ranger or science museum and find out which plants need protection—and don't pick them.

• There's nothing wrong with eating tuna, but the way it's caught isn't good. You have a choice. Even if you like tuna, you might decide you don't want to buy it because you know that catching the tuna might also have killed dolphins. Write to Earth Island Institute, 300 Broadway, Suite 28, San Francisco, CA 94133, for more information.

22. ADOPT AN ANIMAL

Take A Guess.
Why do zoos help endangered animals to have families?
A) They like diapers   B) They want to protect wildlife
C) They like the noise

Elephants, camels, giraffes, penguins, snakes, flamingos, alligators and people—all in the same place. Only at the zoo!

Zoos have always been a place we could go to see lots of different kinds of animals. But today, zoos are doing something else that is very important. They are working to help keep some types of animals alive. Many zoos have an "adopt an animal" program. It's for grown-ups and kids alike.

Did You Know

• Every week, about 20 kinds of plants and animals become extinct—they disappear from the Earth forever! It's a good thing plenty of people are starting to take action.

• Even many of our favorite animals are threatened, like the

Answer: B. And endangered animals need all the help they can get!

panda bear, the rhinoceros, and the African elephant.

• In some zoos, people are trying to save animals by creating areas that look and feel like the animals' real homes.

• At the San Diego Zoo, for example, tigers and Malayan sun bears live in special places that look just like the Asian rainforests they come from.

• In these more natural zoo areas, many rare types of animals—like jaguars and bald eagles—are even able to raise families. That's good news.

• Building special areas and raising babies takes a lot of money. One way zoos are raising this money is through "animal-adoption" programs.

What You Can Do

• "Adopt" an animal. As a "parent," you usually get a fact sheet and photo of your animal (and maybe stickers or pins).

• Most zoos let kids pick what kind of animal they want to "adopt," depending on how much money is donated. Then the money kids send in goes to taking care of that animal.

• It's not cheap— "adoptions" usually start at $25—but maybe you can get an adult to help you. Or share it with a bunch of friends or your whole class at school.

See For Yourself

For more info, write to the American Association of Zoological Parks and Aquariums, 4550 Montgomery Ave., Suite 940N, Bethesda, MD 20814.

23. PET PESTS

Take A Guess.
How many dogs and cats are there in America?
A) 1 million B) Over 10 million C) Over 100 million

Scratch. Scratch. Scratch. It makes you itchy just watching a dog or cat scratch at fleas. And if it's your pet, you want to do something to help.

There are lots of ways to get rid of fleas—like flea collars and flea powders—but many of them are not very good for you, or your pet, or the Earth. That's because they often contain poisons called pesticides.

Pesticides are not terribly safe to make or to use. So it's a good idea for you and your pet to try other things instead.

Did You Know...

• There are 19,000 different kinds of fleas!

• The chemicals we use on our pets to try to get rid of these fleas are sometimes as bad for the pets as they are for the bugs. Some chemicals used on flea collars, for example, are suspected of causing cancer.

• Most fleas don't live on your pet—they live in your house. About 4/5 of them are always hidden in rugs and in the cracks of your floors. So trying to get rid of the fleas on your dog or cat without also doing something to get rid of the fleas in your house doesn't make sense. It won't work.

Answer: C. That's almost half the number of people in America!

What You Can Do

• Give your pet lots of baths with soap and water, which drowns fleas.

• Use a "flea comb" on your pet. This is a special comb with teeth so close together that the fleas get caught in it. Put a jar of soapy water next to you when you do this, and dip the comb in the water whenever you catch a flea. The flea will drop into the water and die.

• If you have fleas jumping around, you might make a flea trap. Put a pan of water on the floor under a lamp. Fleas will fly toward the light, and jump in the water! If you add a teaspoon of dishwashing soap, they won't be able to swim out!

See For Yourself

Go to a pet store and look at all the flea-killers they sell. Look at the labels. You won't be able to understand most of what they say, but you will see a warning on most of them. This means they have some danger-ous chemicals in them. It may be necessary to use them every once in a while in small amounts—but if you can avoid them, it's better for you and your pet.

24. HANG ON TIGHT!

Take A Guess.
Which of these things shouldn't you do with balloons?
A) Celebrate a birthday   B) Decorate at a carnival
C) Feed them to whales

Helium balloons! Big, bouncing, bobbing...Oops! One got away. There it goes, into the sky, getting smaller and smaller...until it's just a speck. Then you blink and it's gone.

Where do helium balloons go? Off into outer space?

Not quite.

Actually, when they lose their helium, they come back to Earth. And that can be a problem for birds and other animals.

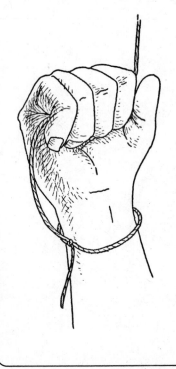

Did You Know

• When helium balloons are released, they are often blown by strong winds into the ocean. Even if the sea is hundreds of miles away, balloons can still land there.

• The salt water in the ocean washes off a balloon's color, making it look clear.

• Sometimes sea creatures think balloons are food and eat them.

• Sea turtles, for example, eat jellyfish—which look and wiggle just like clear balloons. If a

Answer: C. But we do it; helium balloons float to the ocean and get swallowed by whales!

turtle makes a mistake and eats a balloon, the balloon can block its stomach. So the turtle can starve to death.

• Whales sometimes accidentally swallow balloons that are floating in the ocean. The balloons get stuck inside the whale's stomach, and can kill the creature!

• Another hazard: Silver metallic balloons (made of a material called Mylar) sometimes escape from people's hands and get caught in electric power lines. Then they cause the power to go out for many people.

What You Can Do

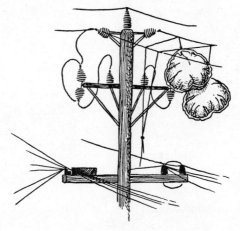

• Try not to let go of your helium balloons.

• Tie them to your wristwatch, your shoe, your wrist, or anything handy.

• If your school plans to let lots of balloons into the air during a celebration, tell them about the dangers to sea animals. Most people don't realize that creatures can be harmed by balloons.

See For Yourself

Test your strength: see how hard you need to pull to break a balloon in two. It probably won't be easy, and you may not be able to do it. That doesn't mean you're weak; it means balloons are made of strong material—another reason why they are so dangerous for sea creatures.

25. EVERY LITTER BIT HURTS

Take A Guess.
Which of these is considered litter?
A) A goose B) A banana tree C) A candy wrapper

Riddle: When is a street like a garbage can?

Answer: When there's litter in it!

That's not very funny, is it? Candy wrappers, soda cans, old newspapers, and other garbage on the ground make it look as though no one cares about the Earth.

But that's not the worst thing about litter. It can also be harmful to animals. It can even kill them.

So every time you get ready to toss out your trash, you have a chance to protect some special creatures.

Did You Know

• Deer and other animals often cut their tongues on half-opened cans.

• Animals are sometimes injured when they eat cigarette butts, plastic wrappers, or Styrofoam.

• Little animals like squirrels sometimes stick their heads in small plastic

Answer: C. Almost anything you throw on the ground and leave there is litter!

containers, trying to get the food that's left, and get stuck there. They die because they can't eat.

• Even an apple core thrown out of a moving car can be dangerous. An animal smelling food can be drawn to the highway and get hit by oncoming traffic.

• How long does litter hang around? It takes a month for a piece of paper to become part of the Earth again. It takes a woolen sock a *year* to do the same thing. And a soda can lying on the ground won't disappear for over *200 years!*

What You Can Do

• Throw garbage in trash cans, not on the ground.

• If you see trash lying on the ground, take time to put it in the garbage.

• When you go for a hike with your friends or family, bring some bags along for trash—the trash you make along the way, as well as the trash you find.

• Organize a "Litter Drive" at school. Get everyone together to make a difference in a park or a playground in your town.

See For Yourself

• For more info on the litter mess, write to Defenders of Wildlife, 1244 19th St., NW, Washington, DC 20036. Ask for their booklet, "Deadly Throwaways."

26. SNIP SIX-PACK RINGS

Take A Guess.
Which of these are you most likely to find on a beach?
A) Zebras B) Six-pack rings C) Trumpet players

W e've all seen plastic six-pack rings—the little plastic circles that hold together six-packs of canned drinks. You probably throw them away as soon as you're done using them, right?
Well, believe it or not, that's just when you can help save the Earth.

Did You Know
• Many six-pack rings wind up in the ocean. Why?
Well, sometimes people leave them on the beach. Other times they are put in garbage dumps near the water, and the wind blows them into the sea.

• Once they're in the water, they are invisible to sea creatures and birds that are hunting for food. And these animals can be hurt—or even killed—by six-pack rings.
• For example: Sea gulls and pelicans can get the rings caught around their necks or beaks when they dive into the water looking for fish. Tangled in the rings, they can drown, strangle, or starve.

76

• Young seals can get the rings caught around their necks when they're little. As they get bigger, the rings get tighter, and the animals choke to death. Even fish, swimming through six-pack rings, sometimes get caught.

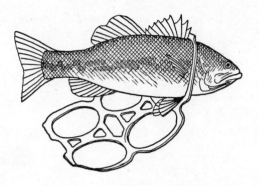

What You Can Do

• Before you toss six-pack rings into the garbage, snip each circle with a scissors (or get someone to help you do it). Once the rings are cut, no animal can get caught on them!

• When you are on the beach, pick up any six-pack rings you find. Snip all the circles, and then throw the rings in a garbage can.

See for Yourself

• Take a trip to your local supermarket. Find the soda and beer cans. Now count the six-packs on the shelves (count them all—no cheating!)

• Imagine that there are stores like this in every town in the

USA…and every one of them uses this many six-pack rings every single day! That's a lot. With this many six-pack rings around, they can be dangerous to ocean animals…even if only a small percentage of them get into the water! So let's start snipping them today!

26. HOME, TWEET HOME

Take A Guess
Where do birds live? A) In nests made of twigs B) In underground burrows C) In milk cartons

Everyone knows that birds build nests. So why should *you* build a house for a bird? One reason is that there often aren't enough trees or grasses in cities for all the birds to make their nests.

Birds all over the world are losing their homes and dying out. Certain birds are already extinct—gone forever, just like the dinosaurs. We need to protect the ones that are left.

You can help a bird family find a place to stay. And you don't need anything fancy, either—just an old milk carton.

Did You Know

• Many birds *migrate*—which means they travel great distances at different times of year: south to warmer weather in the winter, and back north during the summer.

• Some flocks of birds travel 1,800 miles or more! One bird, the Arctic Tern, makes a trip longer than the distance around the Earth!

• If it snows late in spring, after birds have come back north for the summer, they are often left in the cold with nowhere to go. So if you give birds a safe place to nest, they might lay eggs and raise their families right in your own backyard!

Answer: In all of them.

What You Can Do

Build a birdhouse. You can build one out of wood, buy a plastic one…or you can make one out of recycled material, like a milk carton.

The Milk Carton Birdhouse

You'll need:
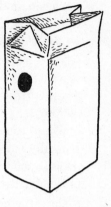
• One empty half-gallon cardboard milk carton
• A pair of scissors
• About two feet of wire—light enough to bend, strong enough to hold the weight of the birdhouse
• Two nails and a hammer
• Dried grass
• Some packing tape (waterproof)

Instructions

• First, completely open up the top of the carton and rinse it out well.
• Take the scissors and cut a hole about the size of a doorknob in one side of the milk carton, a couple of inches below where the top folds. This will be the bird family's "door."
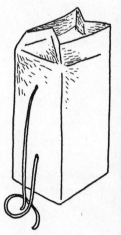
• On the other side of the carton, make two holes— one above the other—with a nail. The top hole should be about 1/3 of the way down from the top. The bottom hole should be 1/3 of the way up from the bottom.
• Now put the wire through the top nail hole, along the inside of the carton, and out the bottom hole.

- Make a bed for the birds by putting some of the dried grass on the carton bottom.
- Close the top of the carton again, and seal it tight with the packing tape.
- Go outside and find a pole or tree. (Try to find one that's not surrounded by other trees, poles, or buildings. Keep it close to home, so you can enjoy it!) Bang the nails in with the hammer, about a foot apart, one above the other.
- Hang the bird house on the nails by wrapping one end of the wire around one nail, and the other end on the other nail. Make sure it's good and tight, so it will stay up. You're done!
- Now wait to enjoy the sights and sounds of bird families in your custom-built birdhouse!

See For Yourself

- Check out a great book called *Birdwise: Forty Fun Feats for Finding Out About Our Feathered Friends*, by Pamela Hickman (published by Addison-Wesley in 1988). It's full of terrific information about birds, how they live and how to live with them.
- If you're interested in making other kinds of birdhouses, write for a free copy of Recycle for the Birds, National Wildlife Federation, 8925 Leesburg Pike, Vienna, VA 22184.

KEEPING THE

THE

EARTH
GREEN

THINKING GREEN

If you look green, you're probably not feeling very well. But if the Earth is green, it's a healthy planet.

A green Earth means that plants are growing. It means that the soil is good, there's plenty of water, the air is clean, animals have places to live and things to eat.

And some wonderful news: Anyone can help keep the Earth green. It's so easy. You can plant a seed, give it some water, and watch it grow. You can save paper so that fewer trees will be cut down. You can "adopt" plants that are already growing and help them enjoy life.

Another important thing about plants (especially trees): They help fight the greenhouse effect and give us oxygen, which is the air we need to live.

What a deal!

We need lots of greenery in our world. Let's start planting!

28. DON'T BAG IT!

Take A Guess.
What's the best kind of bag to use when you go shopping?
A) Plastic B) Cloth C) Paper

Did you ever stop to think how weird it is that everything we buy gets put in bags?...Even when it's only one item, like a candy bar...or a bag of chips? A bag in a bag—now that's crazy!

But it happens all the time. And then we just throw the bag away.

What a waste! Bags are made from the Earth's treasures. Paper bags are made out of trees; plastic bags are made from oil. And manufacturing either of them adds a lot of pollution. But *you* can help. Just say "No" to bags you don't really need.

Did You Know
• If you had a 15-year-old tree and wanted to make paper bags out of it, you would only get about 700 of them.

• How long would they last? In a big supermarket, the clerks could give those bags out with groceries in less than an hour!

• In some other parts of the world, there aren't

Answer: B. Cloth is best; you can use it many times.

enough forests left to make paper bags. So people there have found other ways to carry what they buy. They put their groceries in little carts, or in cloth sacks that they bring from home.

What You Can Do

• Next time you buy something small, tell the clerk you don't need a bag for it. Just say politely, "No thanks, I'd rather have the tree."

• If you don't notice the clerk putting your things in a bag (or if you forget to tell him or her not to), don't be afraid to give the bag back. Say, "Sorry, I really don't need this." Even if the clerk looks at you funny, you'll feel great knowing you're doing the right thing.

• It's cool to bring a bag with you when you go shopping. Use a paper or plastic bag saved from another shopping trip. Or bring a cloth sack or backpack. When the clerk asks you if you want a bag, say, "No thanks, I brought my own. Gotta save the Earth, y' know."

See For Yourself

When you're at the supermarket, watch people leaving the store. Try to count all the bags they've got. Imagine people all over the U.S. leaving supermarkets every day with all those bags. Imagine how many trees are being cut down and how much plastic is used in a single day just for carrying groceries.

29. PLANT A TREE

Take A Guess.
What does an apple tree produce besides apples?
A) Air to help us breathe B) TV shows C) Lemons

Can you think of anything that gives us paper, fruit, nuts, lumber, places for birds and animals to live, places for kids to climb, and *also* helps keep our air clean (now here's the tricky part) *besides* trees?

Think hard; take your time. If you can come up with the right answer, you can help save the Earth.

Are you ready?

The answer is…No. Nothing can take the place of trees—that's why they're so important.

We need to keep the world full of trees. You can help make this happen. You can plant one.

Did You Know

• The average American uses seven trees a year, in paper, wood and other products made from trees. That's over one-and-a-half *billion* trees a year!

• Trees absorb carbon dioxide, a gas that animals and people produce when they exhale. Carbon

Answer: A. All trees (and plants) produce oxygen…and help keep us breathing!

dioxide is also produced by cars and factories, which burn oil and coal.

• Once there wasn't so much carbon dioxide in the air, but today there is too much. Why? There are millions of cars and factories all over the world putting carbon dioxide into the air at the same time, and billions of trees that could have absorbed it have been cut down—so there aren't enough trees left to do the work.

• Trees also provide shade. In hot weather, a house with a few good shade trees next to it is a lot cooler than one without shade trees.

• That house will need much less energy for air conditioning—10% to 50% less!—and that means less coal burned to make energy, which is definitely an Earth-saver!

• Planting a tree is great fun, and one of the best things you can do to save the Earth. The tree will reduce the carbon dioxide in the air, provide beauty and shade and attract wildlife. Every year, you and your tree will grow, proud to know you're *both* helping the Earth.

What You Can Do

• While you're thinking about what kinds of trees to plant, take your family to visit local *botanical gardens* (where lots of different kinds of plants are grown), *arboretums* (a similar kind of place for trees), parks and so on.

• Many of the people who work at or visit these places are very knowledgeable and helpful, and can help you answer questions such as: What kinds of trees grow fast and need little extra water? What kinds attract birds and animals? Talk about this with those tree-lovers and your family.

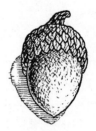

• Go to a local nursery or gardening center with your mom or dad. Talk with the people who work there to figure out what kind of tree to plant...and where. How much space do you have? What kind of soil? What's the weather like?

• Be sure to choose a spot that has the right amount of sunlight, and good soil drainage—too much drainage means the dirt will be too dry, and too little means it'll stay too damp and the tree's roots could rot.

• We don't have enough space here to tell you all the steps to planting a tree. But we do have room to tell you that

planting a tree is a lot easier than you might think. For more tips and some very helpful tree-planting information, contact the folks we've listed under "See For Yourself."

• Think about talking with neighbors,

friends and people at school to see if you can start a community tree-planting effort. You'll be surprised at how many people will love the idea—
especially after you explain just how important trees are and what a good way to save the Earth this is.

See For Yourself

• The best guide to planting trees around cities is called *A Planter's Guide to the Urban Forest*. It's available for $10 from: Tree People, 12601 Mulholland Dr., Beverly Hills, CA 90210. Tree People is a private, nonprofit group that was started by a high school student to plant one million trees in Los Angeles before the 1984 Olympics. When it comes to saving the Earth, it's great to think big!

• The American Forestry Association wants to help Americans plant 100 million trees by 1992 and has a "Global Re-Leaf" program. Write for information: American Forestry Association, Global ReLeaf Program, P.O. Box 2000, Washington, DC 20013; phone (202) 667-3300.

• The National Arbor Day Foundation promotes the celebration of Arbor Day, our national day honoring trees. For more info, such as ideas on celebrating Arbor Day at your school, write: National Arbor Day Foundation, Arbor Lodge 100, Nebraska City, NE 68410.

30. GET GROWING

Take A Guess.
Which of these is easiest to grow indoors on your windowsill?
A) A cabbage patch B) An avocado plant C) A light bulb

Riddle: What is more complicated than a computer, "runs" on water and light instead of batteries or electricity, and even comes in chocolate and vanilla? Here's a big hint—it's green.

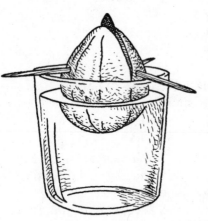

Answer: A plant. (Remember, cocoa beans and vanilla beans come from plants.)

When you think about it, plants are pretty amazing. Every plant, no matter how big or small, helps make our air cleaner and our Earth greener.

Our Earth needs all the help it can get. And you can do something just by planting a seed and adding water! As you take care of it and watch it grow, you can feel good knowing that you're also helping to take care of our Earth.

Did You Know
• Plants, animals and people all need each other. Plants make the oxygen that people and animals breathe; people and animals exhale the carbon dioxide that plants need to live.
• Plants help reduce air pollution by absorbing some pollutants from the air.

Answer: B. You need an avocado pit, a couple of toothpicks and a glass of water.

• Every day bulldozers tear up many plants to make room for more streets, highways, parking lots, homes and businesses.

• If every person in the U.S. planted a couple of seeds, there would soon be more than 250 million more plants growing and making the Earth a healthier place to live.

What You Can Do
Grow some greenery at home!

• Decide what you'd like to grow. Salad greens, flowers, and herbs are easy to grow in containers on a sunny windowsill.

• There are lots of different kinds of salad greens to choose from, such as red leaf lettuce or butter lettuce. The first time you help prepare a salad made with lettuce grown in your very own garden, you'll be so proud! And you'll be amazed at how good and fresh it will taste.

• Lots of herbs used to flavor our food are easy to grow from seeds—like chives, parsley, oregano, dill, and others. Certain flowers are easy too, like alyssum, petunias, or marigolds.

• You can buy the seeds you want at a plant nursery, or even at many hardware stores. While you're there, also buy some potting soil and a little plant food (organic, please!), such as liquid fish emulsion.

• Choose a container to hold the soil. You can actually buy a windowsill planter at the same place you get the other stuff, but there are lots of things you could use to start seeds—a half-gallon milk carton with its top cut off; a large yogurt or cottage-cheese container; or a coffee can. Just be sure the container can hold at least one quart of moist soil, and that you can poke holes in the bottom of it so water can drain out.

• Fill the container to the top with soil. Water the soil to settle it in for the container. The soil should be damp like a wrung-out sponge, but not soggy. Put a dish under the container to catch water that drains out of the soil.

• Plant a few seeds about one inch apart from each other, by placing them on the soil and pushing them under the surface with your finger.

• Be careful to plant them at the right depth. Seeds that are buried too deeply won't sprout. Read the back of the seed package to find out how deep to bury the seeds.

• Pat the soil down gently, and water the soil again, being careful not to disturb the tiny seeds. It's best to use a soft, fine spray of water from a watering can.

• Check the soil every day and keep it moist. If the seeds dry out, they won't sprout.

• When the seeds sprout—when you start to see tiny green stalks and leaves pop through the soil—place the container on a sunny windowsill.

• Once the sprouts (called *seedlings*) have grown a couple of inches high, give the strongest-looking one in each container room to grow, by taking out the other seedlings. With a scissors, snip off the weaker seedlings right at the soil line. (If it seems cruel to you, thank these seedlings for allowing their bigger neighbors to grow; and remember, this happens in nature all the time.)

• Feed your plants about every two weeks with plant food.

• Keep your plants happy by making sure they have enough water, sunlight, and plant food, and they'll make *you* happy by growing into beautiful, healthy plants!

See For Yourself

To find out more about growing plants both indoors and out, check out the book *Kids Gardening: A Kids' Guide to Messing Around in the Dirt* by Kim and Kevin Raftery. It's published by Klutz Press, which is at 2121 Staunton Ct., Palo Alto, CA 94306; phone: (415) 857-0888. Or check your local bookstore.

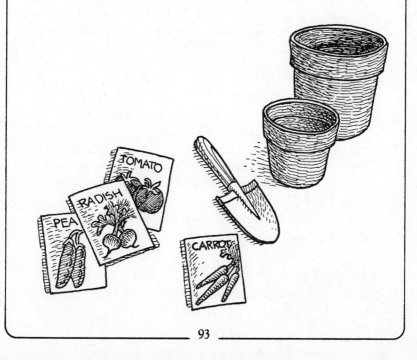

31. BE A
PAPER-SAVER

Take A Guess.
If you stacked up all the paper an average American
uses in a year, the pile would be as tall as. . .
A) A car B) An elephant's eye C) A two-story house

It takes years for a tree to grow enough to be made into
paper. And it takes many forests to make all the paper we
use...and throw away.

Wouldn't it be great if old paper could be turned back into
new paper? Then we'd have more trees and a greener world.

We can make that happen—there *is* a way. We can recycle our paper.

Does that really work? You bet! Want proof? Take a good
look at this book—it's printed on recycled paper!

Did You Know
• Americans use 50 million tons of paper every year, or
about 580 pounds for each person.

Answer: C. Believe it or not, as high as a two-story house!

- How much is that? The paper that four people use in a year weighs as much as a big car.
- To make all that paper, we use more than a *billion* trees!
- If everyone in the U.S. recycled their Sunday newspapers (including the comics), we'd save 500,000 trees every week.
- How is paper recycled? It's shredded and mashed into a glop called pulp, which is then turned back into paper. It's so simple you can do it yourself ! (See Eco-experiments at the end of the book.)

What You Can Do

- You can recycle all kinds of paper—cereal boxes, note paper, bags, newspaper, and so on.
- To start recycling in your house, first find a place where you can put a pile of newspapers and a box for collecting other types of paper.
- Whenever you empty a cereal box, or get ready to toss out a piece of paper, put it in the box instead of the garbage. If you get a newspaper at your house, stack it neatly on the pile every day.
- Don't put shiny paper or paper with plastic attached to it in your box—you can't recycle that stuff.
- Ask a parent to find out where the nearest recycling center is. Maybe your neighborhood has a curbside recycling program. That would really make it easy!
- Every week or two, tie the newspapers into small bundles and take them (and other paper) to the recycling center or put them on the curb for pickup.
- **Extra Tip:** Don't use just one side of a piece of paper—use the other side for scrap paper. That's recycling, too.

See For Yourself

For a free brochure on recycling, write to the Environmental Defense Fund, 257 Park Ave. S. , New York, NY 10010.

32. HELP PROTECT THE RAINFORESTS

Take A Guess.
How much of the rainforests are destroyed every minute?
A) Enough to fill a parking lot B) Enough to fill a movie
theater   C) Enough to fill 50 football fields

Doesn't the word "rainforest" sound exotic and faraway? What does it have to do with you? Why is everyone talking about rainforests now, anyway? What's so important about them?

Tropical rainforests are thick, wet forests that are the homes of amazing people and wonderful animals— like parrots, monkeys and jaguars.

There are so many trees in our rainforests that they actually affect the weather all around the world. They even affect the air we breathe.

In recent years, people have been cutting down the rainforests. This must be stopped, and you can help.

Answer: C. Incredible but true!

Did You Know

• It's estimated that rainforests are being cut down at the rate of about 100 acres per *minute*. That's fast enough to cut down all the world's rainforests in just a few decades.

• Although rainforests cover only a small part of the Earth, they are home to more than half the world's plants and animals—many of which are losing their homes as the forests are cut down.

Why are the rainforests being cut down? For several reasons.

• Farmers cut down trees to clear areas for growing crops. Unfortunately, the soil of the rainforests isn't very good for farming; so a few years later the farmers have to cut down *more* rainforest to continue farming. Before long a whole lot of rainforest is gone, but not much farmland is left behind.

• Ranchers clear rainforests to make pastures for raising cattle. They sell the beef at low prices to the U.S. and other countries. Some fast-food restaurants use this inexpensive beef to make hamburgers.

• In some rainforests, for example in Asia, logging companies cut down large areas of rainforest because some of the trees there are good for lumber. Like the beef we were just talking about, this lumber is then sold to the U.S. and other countries, and made into furniture and other products.

What You Can Do

• Don't buy hamburgers at fast-food restaurants that use beef from cattle raised on land that used to be rainforest. When you go to a fast-food restaurant, ask the people who work there where the beef they use comes from. Explain to them why you're asking.

• Ask your parents not to buy products made out of tropical rainforest wood—rosewood, mahogany, teak, and ebony.

• Learn—and teach!—about the fascinating and wonderful plants, animals and people of the world's rainforests.

• Read books about the rainforests from the library.

• Ask your teacher for lessons on the rainforests.

• Create a "Rainforest Awareness Week" at your school.

• Write a report about the importance of the rainforests.

• Talk with others about the importance of saving the rainforests.

• Write to your U.S. Senators and ask them to help protect the rainforests. Organize a letter-writing campaign at your school. Address your letters to:

(The name of your Senator)
U.S. Senate
Washington, DC 20515

See For Yourself

• You can get an information packet created by high school students, "How to Organize a Rainforest Awareness Week at Your School," from Creating Our Future, 398 North Ferndale, Mill Valley, CA 94941; phone (415) 381-6744.

33. HAVE A LIVING CHRISTMAS TREE

Take A Guess.

*Enough trees are cut down for Christmas each
year in the U.S. and Canada to...*
A) Fill a parking lot   B) Take up 10 city blocks
C) Cover the state of Rhode Island with a forest

Christmas just wouldn't be Christmas without a tree. Where would we put all the decorations and lights? And where would all those great gifts go?

Unfortunately, though, as soon as Christmas is over, the tree dies and gets thrown away.

Too bad!

But hold on! There's a way we can still have Christmas trees without killing them. We can use living Christmas trees.

Did You Know

• Millions of Christmas trees are cut down each year. If people used live Christmas trees instead, there would be that many more trees planted in the U.S. each year.

• In fact, when you think about it, every living Christmas tree does good *twice*: it means one less tree cut down, *plus* one more tree planted.

• You can buy a live Christmas tree in a pot, and plant it in the ground after Christmas, or keep the pot and use it again the next year.

Answer: C. Think of how many trees we'd save if we bought and replanted living trees.

• Many kinds of trees can be used as Christmas trees. Besides the usual ones—pines, firs, and spruces—you can use sequoias (redwoods), cedars, or hemlocks. In fact, just about any kind can be used. Go to your local nursery and pick one out!

• If you don't have the space around your home to plant a tree, call your local park district or city gardening department and ask them where you could plant it. Or maybe you could plant one in a friend's yard, or at school.

What You Can Do

• Go to a nursery or Christmas tree lot and choose a live tree. Keep your tree outdoors until just before Christmas, but be sure to keep it well watered.

• When you bring the tree indoors, put it in a place with plenty of sunlight. Keep it away from heaters and fireplaces: big changes in temperature can cause the leaves or needles to fall off.

• Keep the soil in the pot moist. A tree in a warm room may need water every other day. One easy way to water the tree is to place about a dozen ice cubes on the soil.

• Put something under the pot so the water doesn't drain onto the floor.

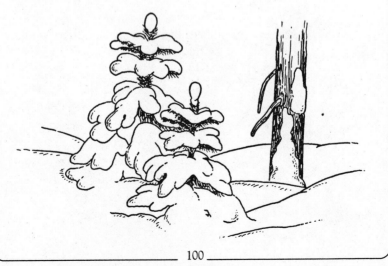

• A week or so after Christmas, remove the decorations and put the tree in a cool place, like a garage, for a couple of days, to get it used to the cold before you put it outdoors.

• Now it's time to plant your tree. If it's very cold where you live, you should probably wait until spring to plant the tree. Just keep it outdoors in a sunny spot, watering it if it gets dry, until spring.

See For Yourself
Next Christmas, go to a Christmas tree lot and count the number of cut trees there. Then think about the many thousands of lots like that in the U.S. It's easy to see there are millions of trees cut down for Christmas every year. Wouldn't you rather have a living Christmas tree?

34. ADOPT A PIECE OF THE EARTH

Take A Guess.

What's the best way to take care of a small patch of grass?
A) Pave it with concrete to protect it B) Pick up the litter
there every day C) Dig a hole in it and bury garbage there

There's probably a little plot of ground in your yard, or in your neighborhood, that can use some loving care. Maybe there are plants that need watering. . .or some ugly litter that needs to be picked up.

Who's going to take care of this little piece of the Earth? Maybe you'd like to "adopt" it for a while.

Did You Know

• Whether you do it alone or with a bunch of people, this really works! Here's a true story:

• At the Washington School in Berkeley, California, the students decided that their schoolyard—a big, ugly blacktop surrounded by an ugly chain link fence—needed a lot of attention.

• With the help of their parents and teachers, they raised money and made plans.

• They divided their schoolyard into three parts. One part was kept as a pavement for playing, one part was made into a maze and a place for wooden play structures, and one part was turned into a nature area.

• In the nature area, kids planted trees, flowers, grass and a vegetable garden. They even made two ponds. Eventually, the ugly metal fence was covered with flowering vines.

• Soon the schoolyard had become a place the students were proud of.

What You Can Do

Walk around your yard, neighborhood or school and find an area that needs some attention. It might be a place that is littered with trash or has no plants on it. Here are some things you could do for your "adopted" bit of earth:

• Pick up litter. Put up signs that say, "Please don't litter."

• Plant some seeds or seedlings to help save the soil.

• Make it nicer to look at by planting flowers. Flowers also attract wildlife (see "Animals in Your Backyard").

• Plant shrubs or trees on your plot to provide food and shelter for birds and squirrels.

• Hang a bird feeder from a pole or tree on your plot to give birds food all year round.

See For Yourself

Can you really help to change things? Take photos or draw pictures of your "adopted" land every couple of months to see. You'll be surprised how important you really are to your little piece of the Earth.

SPENDING ENERGY

WISELY

THOUGHTS ABOUT ENERGY

When I was a kid, my mom used to point out our power plant, a big brick building with three tall smokestacks and lots of big metal wires and machines outside of it. Inside, workers would feed coal to a big fire, and when the coal burned, it released energy that turned into electricity. At the same time, the coal released smoke into the air. As we drove past our power plant, my mom would point to the black smoke and say, "That's the dirtiest plant! We should close it down so it will stop polluting our air!" But back then we didn't know what we would do without the electricity.

We know a lot more now. We know that if we save enough energy, we won't need as many power plants. We also know that the pollution coming from the plant doesn't just smell bad and make people sick, but it hurts the Earth, too. When rain washes the pollution out of the sky, it becomes polluted, acid rain. The acid rain hurts streams and lakes and fish and trees and other natural things that don't even get to use the electricity! (When was the last time you saw a fish watching TV?)

Another thing we have learned is that the pollution is changing the weather all over the planet. Some day, wild animals might be too cold or too hot to survive. Already, some people are doing what they can to save energy so they can help clean up the dirty skies, streams, and land. In this section you will find lots of ways you can, too!

—Karina Lutz,
Home Energy magazine

35. GET A CHARGE FROM BATTERIES

Take A Guess.
Which of these doesn't usually need batteries?
A) A flashlight B) A solar-powered calculator
C) A battery-operated vegetable slicer

Y ou probably play with plenty of battery-operated toys
and other gizmos. After a while, the batteries wear out,
and you have to buy new ones, right?

What do you do with
the old ones?
Just toss them out.
That's not good for
the Earth. Most batteries
contain mercury, a dan-
gerous metal that can
leak into the ground
when the batteries are
thrown away.
Here's some good
news: there is a kind of battery that you don't have to throw
away. It's called a "rechargeable" battery.

Did You Know

• Americans buy two billion batteries every year. That's
about eight batteries for each person in the country—even
counting babies!

• Most of them are made to be thrown away. But "rechargeable" batteries are made to be reused.

• How do they work? When they get run down, you put
them into a little box called a *recharger*.

Answer: B. A solar-powered calculator gets its energy from the sun.

- The recharger plugs into an electrical outlet. Then it takes electricity from the outlet and puts it into the battery.
- After being recharged a while, the battery is ready to use again.
- These batteries aren't perfect—they also contain a dangerous metal called *cadmium*. But they're better for the Earth than mercury batteries, because they can be used many times.

What You Can Do

- Remember that the energy you get from batteries comes from the Earth. Don't waste it: turn your Walkman off if you're not listening to it, make sure your flashlight is turned off before you put it down, and so on.
- Plug in portable tape recorders and radios whenever you can instead of running them on batteries.
- Use things that don't need batteries, like a solar calculator, which runs on light.
- Talk to your parents about getting rechargeable batteries and a recharger. It costs more at first, but if you use lots of batteries, you'll wind up saving money.

See For Yourself

Take a survey in your house. Count up the things you and your family have that run on batteries. Count up the number of batteries that are in them. Now imagine that families all over America have just as many—or more—battery-operated items. Wouldn't it be good for the Earth if all those batteries were reusable?

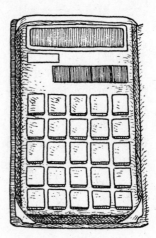

36. LIGHTS OUT!

Take A Guess.
When was the first light bulb invented?
A) Who knows? B) Last year C) Over 100 years ago

A t night, when it gets dark, you flip a switch…and it's light again.

No big deal, right?

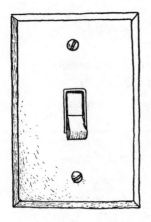

Think again. The energy that powers electric lights comes from the Earth. Being careful about using lights is another way we can help keep our planet healthy.

Did You Know

• Of all the energy that a light bulb uses, how much do you think is actually turned into light? Surprise: Only 1/10! The rest is wasted, because it is turned into heat instead. That's why a light bulb is so hot after it's been on for a little while.

• If a 100-watt bulb is on for half a day, every day, for a year, it can use enough electricity to burn almost 400 pounds of coal. Burning the coal to light the bulb will release nearly a thousand pounds of gases which cause the greenhouse effect, and almost eight pounds of gases that cause acid rain. All that from one light bulb!

• There's an amazing light bulb called a "compact fluorescent" that uses 1/4 of the energy of a regular bulb, and lasts 10 times as long. Wouldn't it be great to put one in your room?

Answer: C. Thomas Edison invented it in 1879.

What You Can Do

• Turn out lights when you're not using them. Whenever you leave a room—and no one else is still there—be sure to flip the switch!

• Use daylight—it's free and doesn't pollute. If you're reading during the daytime, sit near a window. Open the curtains or pull up the blinds or shades.

• Dust some light bulbs. Believe it or not, dusty light bulbs use more energy than clean ones. Ask your folks if you can help save energy—and keep the house clean, too—by dusting light bulbs every once in a while.

• Take a parent or other adult down to the local hardware store to look for compact fluorescent light bulbs. If you can't find one, ask the manager to order them.

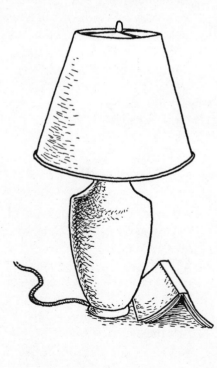

See For Yourself

How many bulbs do people use? Here's a way to get an idea: Walk around your own home, and count up all the bulbs your family uses. Now imagine that there are *100 million* homes like yours, and each of them has the same amount of bulbs. Wow!

37. JOIN THE HEAT-BUSTERS

Take A Guess.
Which of these is a good way to keep warm?
A) A match B) A sweater C) A hot tamale

B r-r-r. You're feeling chilly, so you walk over to the little dial that makes the heater work (the *thermostat*) and you turn it up.

Oh, no! Look out! You turned it up too far! You've just let out…
The Heat Monster !

Here it comes, pouring out of the heater vents, eating up energy as it spreads around your home, making the air hotter and hotter.

But wait! There is something you can do to stop it.

Quickly, you turn down the heat…And the Heat Monster disappears!

Congratulations! You've just joined the Heat-Busters.

Did You Know

• Almost half of the energy you use in your home is spent on heating it.

• If everyone in America turned their heat down six degrees, we'd save 500,000 barrels of oil *each day*.

• If we used less oil, we wouldn't need so many big oil tankers—and there would be less chance of another giant oil spill like the one that happened in Alaska.

• When we use less oil for heat,

Answer: B. A sweater will keep you warm indoors, so you won't have to turn up the heat.

we're fighting the greenhouse effect. Every year, heating U.S. homes puts over a *billion* tons of "greenhouse gases" into the air. We can reduce that by turning down the heat.

What You Can Do

• In the winter, keep the heat as low as you comfortably can.
• Instead of running around the house in a T-shirt and bare feet during the winter (and turning up the heat to keep warm), you can help the Earth by dressing warmly. (Yes, even indoors.) It's a great idea to put on a sweater, for example. It keeps you warm and keeps the heat down.
• **With a parent:** If you've got a furnace, volunteer to help check the air filter. That's the screen that keeps dirt out of furnace.
• If the filter gets clogged with dirt, your heater has to work harder—which means it's spending too much energy to keep you warm. Air filters have to be changed about once a month.

See for Yourself

How warm is warm enough? Find out how low you can set your thermostat and still feel comfortable. Start by setting it five degrees lower than usual, and put on a sweater or sweatshirt. If you get too warm after 10 or 15 minutes, turn the heat down another few degrees. On the other hand, if you're not warm enough (and putting on a heavier sweater won't do the trick), you can try setting the thermostat up just a degree or two. That's still several degrees lower than it was before!

38. STAY OUT OF HOT WATER

Take A Guess.
Where does the hot water in your house come from?
A) Clouds B) Hot water factories
C) The water heater

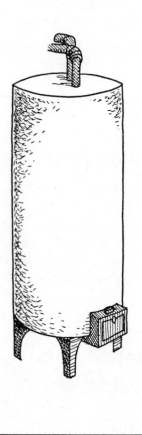

If people from long ago saw our faucets, they'd say, "Hot water right out of the tap? Amazing!"

It used to take them a lot of time and energy to get hot water. People had to collect wood, light a fire, tend the fire,...and then they had finally had hot water!

What a difference it is today!

Now hot water is so easy to get that we let it run down the drain without even thinking. That's not a very good habit, because it still takes a lot—though a different kind—of energy to heat our water.

Did You Know
• The water supplied to your home is cold water—like the water in rivers, lakes and wells, which is where drinking water comes from.

• A pipe carrying water to your home comes into the building and branches in two. One branch takes water to all the *Cold* faucets in your house. The other branch

Answer: C. The water heater.

goes to the hot water heater, a big tank that holds between 20 and 50 gallons. The heater goes on and stays on until the water gets hot.

• How does it know when to turn itself off? A little gadget called a thermostat checks the temperature and "tells" it.

• Now the hot water sits there, waiting to be used. When you turn the *Hot* faucet, hot water starts flowing out of the tank. It keeps flowing until you turn the faucet off.

• When hot water leaves the water heater, cold water takes its place. The thermostat "sees" that the water is getting too cold, so it turns on the heat again.

• This happens over and over and over, every day, even while you sleep: if the water gets cold, the heater turns on... even if no one's using hot water!

• It's easy to see why it takes so much energy to heat water!

What You Can Do

• We talked about not wasting water by leaving it on in "Presto, on!...Presto, off!" Now we'll remind you to be a little extra careful when it comes to using *hot* water.

• By saving hot water, you save two treasures of the Earth at one time—water and energy.

• When you take a bath or a shower ...when you wash your hands or face...when you're washing dishes... whenever you use hot water, remember: you have a chance to help save the Earth by using it wisely.

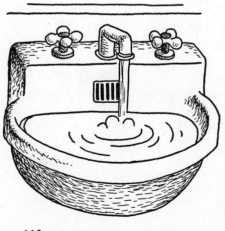

39. IF IT'S NOT FAR, DON'T TAKE THE CAR

Take A Guess.
What do you think causes more pollution?
A) Fireplaces   B) Cars   C) Steamships

Need to go somewhere? Down to the store...over to a friend's house...out to a movie? The easiest thing to do is get a ride in the car.

But that's not the best thing for the Earth.

Cars create pollution, so the less we drive, the healthier our planet will be.

Sure, it may take you a little longer to get where you're going....But isn't clean air and water worth the extra effort?

Did You Know

• There are more cars in America than anywhere else in the world—140 million of them!

• Every year American cars drive a trillion miles. How many is that? Well, it would take you your whole life just to *count* that high!

Answer: B. Cars are some of the biggest polluters in the world!

• When these millions of cars burn up gas, they produce something called "exhaust." It is one of the worst things for the Earth.

• "Exhaust" contains invisible gases that add to the greenhouse effect, acid rain, and smog.

• Bicycles don't make exhaust—they don't pollute. So if you already ride a bike, you're already saving the Earth.

• In other countries, more people ride bikes instead of cars. In Japan, for example, there are special parking garages for bicycles, so people can ride them to work.

What You Can Do

• Next time you need to go somewhere, think twice before you ask for a ride. Is it close enough to walk? Can you ride your bike?

• Encourage your parents to walk or bike instead of riding. Suggest that you can walk or bike together!

See for Yourself

Here's a fascinating experiment. You'll need an adult to help.

Step 1: Get an old white sock. Put it over the tailpipe of your car. (Only do it if the tailpipe is cool; if the car's been running recently, wait until it cools down!)

Step 2: Get an adult to turn on the car and let it run for one minute. Then turn the car off.

Step 3: Ask the adult to take the sock off the car, and hand it to you.

Step 4: Examine the sock. It will be full of pollution that is normally invisible to us.

Step 5: Imagine what is being put into the air by the millions of cars that run for hours every day. Aren't you glad you ride a bike?

40. STOP THE GREAT ESCAPE!

Take A Guess.

Where does most heat escape from your house?
A) *The telephone*   B) *The TV*   C) *The windows*

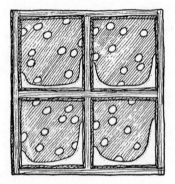

Right now, in your home, there's a great escape going on! Air is sneaking out around windows and doors—and in the winter, that's a crime! It costs us a lot to keep our homes warm. So we've got to catch the air before it gets out.

Did You Know

• More than half the energy we use at home is for heat. And half of *that* is wasted!

• This means that with the energy we now spend heating one home, we could actually heat two of them! It's true!

• How does the heat escape? Under doors, around window frames, through the attic, up the chimney....It can even go right through glass windows, especially if they're broken.

• By keeping even a little heat from being lost, you are helping fight the greenhouse effect and acid rain...and saving oil, coal and other treasures of the Earth that get used for heat.

What You Can Do

• Pull down the window shades at night and close the curtains when it's cold. This makes a "wall" that helps keep heat inside.

Answer: C. The cracks around windows and doors are big energy-wasters.

• Make sure the windows in your room are closed tightly on cold nights. And make sure any broken windows get fixed!

• If your parents want to put up weatherstripping, ask if you can help.

• Go to the store with them and learn about all the different kinds you can buy. Then, take it home and help save energy by helping to plug up the leaks!

See For Yourself
Go on a "Leak Hunt."

• On the next cold, windy day, take a 6-inch piece of ribbon or a piece of light paper around to all the windows and doors you want to check.

• Hold the ribbon or paper up to the places where the air might be escaping; if the ribbon or paper moves, you've found a leak.

• Make a map showing the leaks and give it to your parents. What an eco-detective!

41. KEEP IT COOL

Take A Guess.
Which uses more electricity?
A) A radio B) A refrigerator C) A toaster

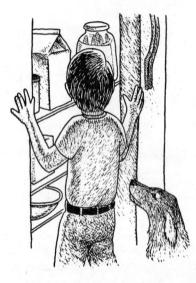

What is an icebox? Back in the old days, before electricity and refrigerators, everyone had a box in the kitchen where they put a big hunk of ice. That's how they kept their food cold.

But didn't the ice melt? It sure did. So every week an ice man came by to sell more ice.

It wasn't nearly as easy as it is today. On the other hand, it didn't use up the Earth's resources the way refrigerators do.

So do you think you can convince your parents to get rid of your refrigerator and get an icebox instead?

Ha! No way! But here are some things you *can* do with your refrigerator.

Did You Know

• We open our refrigerators almost 22 times a day. That's over 8,000 times a year for each one!

• When you open the refrigerator, the cold air you feel coming out is trading places with hot air going in. That means the fridge is getting warmer inside, and has to use lots of extra electricity to cool back down.

Answer: B. Refrigerators are on all day, every day of the year! We never turn them off.

- When a refrigerator is full of food, it needs less electricity to keep cold, because the food soaks up the cold air and keeps it trapped inside.

- There's a dial inside the fridge for adjusting its temperature. But many people don't know it, so refrigerators often wind up colder than they need to be.

- The "coils" —those things that look like tubes—on the back or bottom of the fridge are important. They help keep your refrigerator cold by taking the heat out from the inside. But they don't work well when they're dusty.

What You Can Do

- Don't open your refrigerator unless you have to. Once you've opened it, quickly get what you want and close the door. Think about what you want *before* you open it.

- If your folks say it's okay, make it your job to keep the coils free of dust. Brush the coils off with a broom, dustcloth, or (with their permission) vacuum cleaner.

- With a parent, check to see if your refrigerator is colder than necessary. It should be set between 38°and 42°. If you raise the temperature a little, the food will still stay chilled but you'll use less electricity. Hint: Feel the food. If it's icy, the dial is set way too cold.

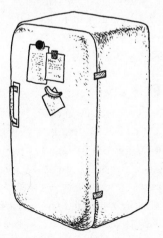

See For Yourself

Keep a record of how many times you open the refrigerator during the day. Are you opening it more than you really need to? And how long do you keep it open?

42. WHAT'S COOKING?

Take A Guess.
What is the fastest way to boil a pot of water?
A) Leave the lid on B) Insult it C) Make it angry

Congratulations! You're finally old enough to use the stove or microwave—your mom or dad said that *you* can turn it on by yourself!

Stoves use a lot of energy. And when you're old enough to use the stove, you're also old enough to know how to save energy with it.

What if you're still waiting for your folks to decide whether you're old enough? Well, in the meantime, you can teach *them* a few energy-saving cooking tips.

Did You Know

• Every time you open an oven door to see what's cooking, 25° to 50° of heat go flying out the door. That's a lot!

• When hot air escapes from the oven, more electricity or gas is needed to heat the oven back up again. That means energy—and money—wasted.

• More than half the homes in the U.S. now have microwave ovens. Do you? If used properly, microwaves need a lot less energy than regular ovens. Toaster ovens use less energy

Answer: A. Leaving the lid on creates heat much faster.

than ovens, too.

• A covered pot of water boils faster than an uncovered pot, so it uses less energy to reach the boiling point.

• You can use up to 25° less heat if you bake with glass or ceramic (clay) pans. They keep in more heat than other pans.

What You Can Do

• Put a cover on your pot when you're boiling water.

• The bottom of your pot should be the same size as the burner you're cooking on.

• Leave the oven door closed while you're baking.

• Listen to your food and pots while you're cooking. If you hear whistles, screams, loud sizzles, or other weird noises you're not used to, the heat may be turned up too high.

See For Yourself

• Fill two pots with the same amount of water. (Measure it out with a measuring cup.) Cover one pot; leave the other uncovered. Start the heat on both of them at the same time. Be sure the heat is set at the same level. See which boils first. Why? Which uses more energy?

SPREADING

THE WORD

WORDS AND THOUGHTS

EcoKid power is all over the USA. It's your cousins. It's your friends. It's you. What can EcoKid power do? Plenty! You just have to know how to turn it on! When you write a letter to the president that says, "Ban ivory! I want elephants around when I grow up!" show it to your friends. They'll want to write to the president, too. When you decide not to buy food that comes in Styrofoam, tell other kids. They'll stop buying Styrofoam, too. When you want to learn more about the ozone hole or acid rain, ask your teacher a question. Other kids will want some answers, too. And when your friends tell you what they're doing to spread the word, help *them* by spreading it, too.

The most important thing for you to remember is that numbers count. There are millions of kids, and if you all act, then all of you count. All of you can make a difference. And by the way, if you're finding lots of ideas you like in this book, you can bet other kids are finding them, too. It's your world. Saving it is up to you, too. The more kids who know, the more they can do.

—Randi Hacker & Jackie Kaufman,
P-3 magazine

43. TEACH YOUR PARENTS WELL

Take A Guess.
Do parents care about the Earth?
A) Of course B) Only on Tuesdays C) They're too old

P SSTT! Want to know a secret?
Your parents really care what you think…even though
they sometimes pretend not to.
So here's a chance to help save the Earth by teaching
them some important things they may not know.

Did You Know
• When your parents were kids, hardly anyone ever worried
about saving the environment. That's because they didn't

know it was in trouble.

• They developed some bad
habits. They made as much
garbage as they wanted; they
wasted energy whenever they
wanted; they used up the
Earth's treasures, just for fun.

• Today, they know better—
but they still have a lot of bad
habits. That's because it's
hard to change the way you
do things after you grow up.

What You Can Do
• Gently share some of the things you've learned with your
parents or other grown-ups. Don't nag them or bug them

Answer: A. Of course they do!

—just tell them a few facts about the environment every once in a while. They'll be very interested.

• Show them by doing. Be a good example for them. If you want to get recycling started in your home, for instance, the best way to get your parents involved is by doing it yourself. When they see it really means something to you, they'll pitch in.

• Talk to them about your concern for the future—how important it is that they help take care of the Earth so it will still be healthy when you get older.

• Compliment them when they do something good for the Earth. Tell them you appreciate it. Everyone likes to feel they're doing the right thing.

• Read about the Earth together. For example: Share your latest copy of *P-3*. Grown-ups will learn something from it.

• Most of all, remember this: You and your parents and everyone else are in this together. Help each other, so that you can all help the Earth.

See For Yourself

We mentioned *P-3* above. Have you heard of it? It's a great kids' environmental magazine—fun, creative, and informative…We can't say enough good things about it. Try it! Subscriptions are $14.00. Write to: to: *P-3*, P.O. Box 52, Montgomery, VT 05470.

P.S.: "P-3" stands for "Planet-3"—Earth, the third planet from the sun.

44. MAKE NEWS

Take A Guess.
Which of these is the easiest to write a letter with?
A) A piece of chalk B) A pencil C) A hammer

Extra! Extra! Read all about it!
Where? In the newspaper.
Would you like to tell everyone what you think about saving the Earth? Why not write a letter to your local newspaper?

Did You Know

• Every day, 62 1/2 million newspapers are printed in America.

• Most of them have a special section called "Letters to the

Editor." These letters are written to the newspaper by readers who have ideas they want to share.

• The newspapers print the letters because they feel it is important for people to voice their opinions.

• Usually, the letters are written by adults. But every once in a while, a kid will write. When that happens, people pay special attention to it; kids have a special way of looking at the world.

What You Can Do

• Write a letter to your local paper. Tell them what you're

Answer: We're not telling. But please don't try to write a letter with a hammer.

doing to save our world. Or tell them what you wish everyone would do—and why.

• Start the letter with "Dear Editor." And when you finish it, be sure to add your name and address and phone number.

• Ask an adult to help you get the newspaper's address. Usually, you can find it on the "Letters to the Editor" page.

• If the newspaper doesn't print your letter, don't give up. Keep writing. The more times you write, the more chances there are that one of your letters will be printed.

• If that happens, many people will be able to read it. And they'll learn something important about saving the Earth.

At School: Suggest that your class write to the newspaper.

• You can have a discussion about saving the Earth.

• Then you can write a group letter together and sign it "From the __ class at ___ school."

• Or each person can write her or his own letter and your class can send them all together.

45. GET SCHOOL-WISE!

Take A Guess.
What's a good way to save the Earth at school?
A) Recycle paper B) Recycle glass C) Share information

Where can you start working to change the world? Why not start with your school? That's one place where you *know* they'll listen to kids. And since schools spend millions of dollars every year on paper, books and other supplies, kids can have a say in what they do.

So getting people at your school to begin saving the Earth is one of the *best* things kids can do together.

Did You Know

• Schools spend billions of dollars on supplies every year. That means they can help to save the world by buying things that are good for the Earth. Unfortunately, most of them aren't doing this. Fortunately, you can change that— and the savings (to the Earth) will start adding up!

• Schools buy more books than anyone else in the country. And yet hardly any textbooks are printed on recycled paper.

• Schools buy millions of pounds of writing paper every year. Very little of it is recycled.

Answer: All of them! There are many Earth-positive things you can do at school.

• Schools buy millions of pounds of paper towels, toilet paper, napkins and so on. Are they made of recycled paper?

What You Can Do

• Everyone in school can write to textbook publishers and ask them to print on recycled paper. Point out the benefits to the environment, and that it's good to teach kids by example, as well as by the words in the books.

• Ask your principal and teachers to use only recycled paper. Write to the Earth Care Paper Co. for their catalog of good-for-the-Earth paper products and show it to the principal.

• Do you use computers in your class? You can use recycled computer paper.

• Use *unbleached* disposables. Many paper goods are bleached to make them white, which can create pollution in streams and rivers.

• Put together a fact sheet with your class (base it on things you've learned from this book and from other organizations), and pass it around the school, so kids will know what they can do. Be sure to put it on recycled paper!

See For Yourself

• The Earth Care Paper Co. sells recycled paper products by mail. Write to them for a catalog: Earth Care Paper, PO Box 3335, Madison, WI 53704. Ask for a few extra copies for your principal and teachers.

46. START A RECYCLING PROGRAM

Take A Guess.
What's the best thing to do with a used soda can?
A) Eat it for lunch B) Wear it on your head C) Recycle it

W e've talked about ways to recycle and precycle, save energy, and do other things to help save the Earth at home. But where's the other place you and other kids spend most of your time?

That's right: at school. Every day there are dozens—in some places, hundreds or thousands—of kids at each school...plus the adults who work there. And there are thousands of schools in this country. Imagine how much good all those people can do for the Earth if they try!

One really great way to get your school and all the people in it involved in saving the Earth is to start a School Recycling Center.

Did You Know

• Every day at your school, hundreds of pieces of paper are

used. Unless you already have a recycling center there, all that paper will get thrown away.

• Your school cafeteria probably provides over 1,000 cartons of milk every week. That's an awful lot of paper! Is it thrown away...or recycled?

• Does anyone drink out of aluminum cans at school? Do you get cans of juice in the cafeteria?

Answer: B. Wear it on your head, of course. Just kidding.

Maybe the teachers' lounge has a a soft-drink machine that uses cans. The school may also use aluminum foil. All that aluminum can be recycled!

• Cafeterias often use food supplies that come in very large tin cans. Those cans can be recycled just like cans of pet food at home.

• Don't forget glass. Jars and bottles that can't be reused can always be recycled.

What You Can Do

• Tell your teacher you'd like to start a recycling center. This would make a terrific class project for an environmental sciences class.

• You could even have a contest among different classes, to see which one comes up with the most fun and interesting ways to get the whole school to recycle.

To have a recycling center at your school, you'll need some special things:

• Several large, sturdy cardboard boxes or bins to collect the glass, metal and paper. Remember: don't leave the boxes out where they'll get wet!

• A place to put recycled materials that is easy to get to but not in the way.

• Signs that say what kind of material goes into each bin…and what to do with them. For instance: You want to remind people to be extra careful with glass, so you don't wind up with a lot of broken glass on the ground! And you will want to remind people to take the caps or lids off jars and bottles before putting them in the bins.

• Here's something very important: You'll need a way to get the recycled materials to your town's recycling center. If you don't collect too much stuff, and somebody's parents can lend a car or truck, you can organize a recycling pick-up day—say a Saturday morning—when a group of kids go to school and help bring it all to the recycling center.

• Maybe your area has "curbside pick-up." In that case, all you have to do is make sure the bins are out on the sidewalk the day before pick-up day. Call your local city government for more information. (If you don't have "curbside pick-up," you could make a project out of getting your town to start it!)

Make It Work!

Once you have the school recycling center set up, be sure to let everyone know about it.

• Make posters announcing the center. It could be a great project for art class.

• An announcement could be sent out to local newspapers, and radio and TV stations. You might even find your school on TV!

• How about other schools? There could even be a friendly contest between schools to see who can recycle the most or have the most fun doing it!

Share the News!

Renew America is an organization that collects stories about people who help create Earth-positive change in their communities. If your recycling center is a big success, then tell them about it. Everyone should share their good news! Write to: Renew America
1001 Connecticut Avenue NW, Suite 1719
Washington, DC 20036

47. KEEP AN EYE ON THE SKY

Take A Guess.
Which of these has contributed to the ozone hole?
A) Styrofoam B) Aerosol cans C) Refrigerators

At the beginning of this book, we talked about the ozone hole. We haven't really mentioned it since. That's *not* because the ozone hole isn't important; really, it might be the most important issue people have to face.

But our disappearing ozone layer is not an easy problem to solve. It's going to take work, and cooperation. We have to do it together.

Will you help?

What You Can Do

• The ozone layer is mainly being damaged by CFC gases in things like air conditioners, refrigerators, insulation, and fire extinguishers.

• We don't think adults would keep on making these gases if they realized they were harming all life on Earth.

• If kids speak up—kids like you, your friends, and your classmates—and remind adults that they need to make a big change, right now, before it's too late, then you'll be accomplishing something important.

• So spread the word about the ozone hole! That's one way kids can save the Earth!

Answer: All. But they're experimenting with new chemicals that won't hurt the ozone.

48. WRITE TO WORLD LEADERS

Take A Guess.
How do you start a letter to the President?
A) Hi! B) Dear Mr. President C) Hey, you!

Will you ever talk to the President of the United States? How about the Prime Minister of Canada? Maybe you'll never talk to them in person, but you

can still let them know what you think about saving the Earth.

How? You can write them a letter! Presidents, senators, and other leaders need to hear from people like you to help them make important decisions about our planet. You can write on your own...or you can write with your whole class at school!

Stand up and speak out for our great planet Earth!

What You Can Do

• Write to the American leader. Send your letter to: President George Bush, The White House, Washington DC 20501

• Write to the Russian leader. Send your letter to: General Secretary Mikhail Sergeyevich Gorbachev, Secretariat of the CPSU, Central Committee, Staraya Ploshchad 4, Moscow, 103132, The U.S.S.R.

• Write to the Japanese leader. Send your letter to: Prime Minister Toshiki Kaifu, Nagata-Cho, Chiyoda-Ku, Tokyo, 100, Japan.

Answer: B. "Dear Mr. President" is considered the proper way to start a letter.

See For Yourself

• If you want to write to a world leader, and don't know where to find the address, write to the person's embassy at the United Nations, United Nations Plaza, New York, NY 10017.

• You can find the addresses of people you'll want to write to about the topics you care about in *P3, The Earth-based Magazine for Kids*, P.O. Box 52, Montgomery, VT 05470. Write for info on how to get their latest issue.

• If you want to write to a U.S. Senator, send a letter to Senator _____, U.S. Senate, Washington, DC 20510. Reach your Representative at the U.S. House of Representatives, Washington, DC 20515.

• Is there someone else in the government you'd like to write to? If you aren't sure where to send your letter, contact 20-20 Vision, 69 South Pleasant St. #203, Amherst, MA 01002. They're a wonderful organization that can help you track down government officials' addresses.

49. GET INVOLVED

Take A Guess.
How many organizations are trying to save the Earth?
A) None B) Three or four C) Hundreds

I f you really care about the Earth, and you wish that you could be doing something with other people who feel the same way, what should you do?

Well, you could walk around with a sign that says, "I care about our Earth, please talk to me."

Or you could stop everyone you meet on the street and try to  talk to them about saving the Earth.

But there's an easier way: You could get involved with environmental organizations. These are groups made up of people who—like you—are concerned with what's happening to the Earth. They work hard to protect it all the time, and they're always looking for folks to join them.

Who Are They?
Some of these organizations have special interests—like saving animals or preserving the ocean or planting trees. Others are interested in everything that has to do with the future of our environment. All of them are very important, and all of them are worth knowing about.

Answer: C. There are hundreds of groups dedicated to saving our Earth!

What You Can Do

• Here is a list of some environmental groups. There are many more than we can include here. A number of them are listed in our book, *50 Simple Things You Can Do to Save the Earth*. If you're looking for more groups to contact, we recommend that you look at the "Stay Involved" section in it.

• You can write and see if they have any special programs for kids. If they don't, why not suggest that they start one? Sometimes, that's all it takes to get them going.

See For Yourself

The Natural Resources Defense Council
40 West 20th Street
New York, NY 10011
They're starting a kids' environmental organization—ask them about it!

The Environmental Defense Fund
1616 P Street NW, Suite 150
Washington, DC 20036

Renew America
1001 Connecticut Avenue NW, Suite 1719
Washington, DC 20036
They've got an interesting collection of environmental "success stories"—true stories about kids who made a difference.

Greenpeace
1436 U Street NW
Washington, DC 20009

50. DREAM A BETTER WORLD

This was written by Gideon Javna, age nine.

I like to imagine what it would be like if we had no environmental problems. I imagine a beautiful world. The air is clean, there is no such thing as Styrofoam. I imagine I wake up in my own house, eat my usual foods. But while I'm walking to school, I realize that the air seems clean. In school, the water I wash my hands with is clean. When I ask my teacher about pollution, she says there is no such word. I also ask her about the Alaskan oil spill. She says there were never any oil spills. I can't believe it. I ask my friend to pinch me so I can wake up. Then I do wake up. But I want the world to be like my dream.

This was written by John Javna, age forty.

I'm Gideon's uncle and I'm about to be a dad for the first time. I am very excited. But I wonder what the world will be like for my child. Will he or she be able to enjoy the beautiful blue sky and the sound of the ocean at the beach?. . . Or be able to walk in the woods?. . .Or be able to listen to birds singing on a still day? I hope so. That is my dream.

Dreams are the way we decide what we want. We imagine something. . .and then we make it happen. It is an amazing part of being a human being.

So if you care about saving the Earth—and I know you do—then keep dreaming. Let your imagination show you which way to go. Dream a better world.

ECO-

EXPERIMENTS

Eco-Experiment #1
BACK TO THE EARTH

Some things are "biodegradable"—which means they eventually break down and go back to the Earth. But which things are, and which aren't? This will help you figure it out.

What You'll Need
- An apple core
- A leaf of lettuce
- Some plastic packaging
- A piece of Styrofoam
- A small shovel

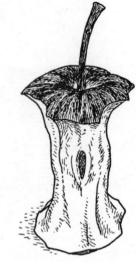

What To Do
1. Find a spot where it's okay to dig a few holes.

2. Dig four holes. Each one should be wide and deep enough to put something in.

3. Put the apple core in one hole, the lettuce in the next, the plastic in another, and the Styrofoam cup in the fourth hole.

4. Fill the holes back in with dirt.

5. Mark the spots where you've buried your four things. Make sure you'll be able to find them again.

6. Wait a month, then go back and dig them up.

7. You'll have no trouble finding the plastic and Styrofoam, but the lettuce and maybe the piece of apple will be gone.

What You Discover

• The lettuce and apple core are biodegradable; they can become part of the Earth again. They're in the soil where they can help grow more apples, or grass, or lettuce. (Note: depending on where you dug your holes, it may take longer for the apple and lettuce to turn into soil. The warmer and moister the ground is, the quicker it will happen.)

• But the plastic packaging and Styrofoam are still there. They are made from the Earth's resources, but we have changed them into something that cannot become a part of the Earth again.

• Which of these is better for us…and our planet? Are we taking too many things out of the Earth that can't be put back? Is it important for us to change?

Eco-Experiment #2
IT CAME FROM UNDERGROUND

*We talked about pure, fresh underground water
becoming polluted. Here's a demonstration of
what can happen to us—and other living
things—when it does.*

What You'll Need
- A glass of water
- A stick of fresh celery with the leaves still on it
- Some red or blue food coloring.

What To Do
1. Carefully cut off the bottom of the celery.

2. Put a couple of drops of food coloring into the glass. Pretend that this is pollution. Watch it spread out in the glass until all the water turns the same color. That's how pollution spreads.

3. Put the celery in the glass. Pretend that this is a little plant, a tree, or even a person who drinks water from the ground. Let the celery stalk sit there for a few hours

4. After a few hours, go back and check out the celery. Cut it and you'll be able to see how the "polluted" water has moved up through the stalk.

What You Discover
• By "polluting" the water, we also "polluted" the plant. Clearly, whatever we do to our water, we do to ourselves and all other living things. A plant that gets its water from the ground will also drink the pollution in the water; a person who gets his or her water from the ground also is exposed to pollution. Since we can't avoid it, we have to prevent it.

Eco-Experiment #3
SMOG PATROL

It's easy to talk about air pollution, but much harder to imagine what it's doing to things, plants, and people. This experiment will help you see what it actually does.

What You'll Need
- Eight natural rubber bands
- Two coat hangers
- A plastic bag
- A magnifying glass

What To Do

1. Bend each coat hanger into a rectangle

2. Slide four rubber bands onto each coat hanger, making sure they're stretched tight. If they're not tight at first, bend the coat hangers out until they are.

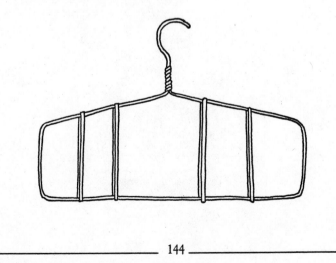

3. Hang one up outside in a shady place so it's out of the sun. That's important.

4. Put the other coat hanger in a plastic bag, and seal it tightly. Keep it indoors in a drawer.

5. Wait a week.

6. When a week is up, check out the rubber bands you hung outside. Are they cracked and broken? Use the magnifying glass to look them over carefully.

7. Compare the rubber bands you hung outside with the ones you kept in the bag by stretching each group the same distance. Do you notice any difference?

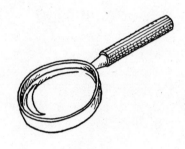

8. If the rubber bands from outdoors are still in good shape, hang them back up and keep them there for a few more weeks. See what happens to them over a longer time.

What you discover

If you live in a place where the air is clean, it will take a long time for rubber bands to show damage. But if you live in an area where the air is very polluted, the rubber bands will break in a few weeks. That's because, unseen by you, smog— air pollution—has been eating away at them.

Polluted air is bad for all things on the Earth. It hurts animals, trees, farmers' crops and even people in the same way it damaged your rubber bands. That's why we need to stop it.

Eco-Experiment #4
RAINDROPS KEEP FALLING ON MY HEAD

You've read about acid rain and the harm it can do to fish and forests. Here we'll see what it can do to plants.

What You'll Need
- Three 1-quart jars with lids
- Measuring cups
- Three small potted plants that you're willing to sacrifice in the name of science
- A bottle of vinegar or lemon juice
- Six short strips of masking tape to use as labels
- A pen or marker

What To Do
1. Make two labels that say "a little acid."

2. Measure 1/4 cup of vinegar or lemon juice into one jar, and fill it up the rest of the way with cold water from the tap.

3. Put one of the labels that says "a little acid" on the jar. Put the other on one of the pots. You will use the mixture in this jar to water this plant.

4. Make two labels that say "a lot of acid." Repeat steps 2 and 3, but this time put a *full* cup of vinegar or lemon juice in the jar.

5. Write "tap water" on the last two labels. Put one on the last pot, and the other on the last jar. Fill the last jar just with water.

6. Set the plants next to each other, so they get the same amount of sunlight.

7. Whenever the plants need water (every 2 to 4 days), water each one with water from the jar that matches its label. See how long it takes for the effects of the acid to set in. What do you notice about the plants? How do they differ in color?

What You Discover

The more acid in the plant water, the sooner they die. This is an illustration of what happens in nature when acid rain falls. It happened faster in your experiment than in nature, because you watered your plants with a stronger acid than most of the rain that falls in this country. (That way, you could see the results faster.) But rain is becoming more acidic all the time. We need to keep it from getting worse.

Eco-Experiment #5
BE A JUNK FOOD DETECTIVE

When you go to your favorite fast-food restaurant and order a burger and french fries, do you think about what comes with them? We don't mean the pickles, onions, and special sauce—we mean the wrappers, bags, and other things you'll throw away. Let's take a look.

What You'll Need
- A few friends
- Some money to buy lunch
- A list of fast-food restaurants you can walk or ride your bike to

What To Do
1. To do this experiment right, you'll need to get fast-food from several restaurants.

• To make this easy (and as cheap as possible), each person in your group will buy her or his lunch at a different restaurant.

• Buy about the same thing at each restaurant. Then you can really compare sandwiches with sandwiches, cold drinks with cold drinks, and dessert with dessert.

2. Okay, now go buy the food. Take it with you from restaurant to restaurant, but keep the food from each restaurant separate.

3. After you go to the last restaurant, take all the bags of food home and eat lunch. But don't throw the paper wrapping, cups, napkins, salt, plastic forks or spoons, Styrofoam hamburger carton, french fries containers, and all the other garbage away. Put it aside and—this is important—keep the stuff you got from each restuarant separate.

4. Now sort through it all. Figure out which restaurants sold you the most garbage with your lunch. Figure out which ones sold you the least. Are you surprised at how much there is? Imagine that millions of people buy the same food—and get the same garbage—every single day. What a mess! What a waste!

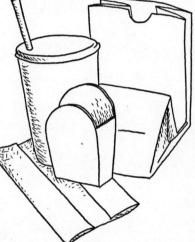

What You Discover

We create a lot of garbage, even when we don't mean to. That's one of the big reasons we're running out of places to put it. But what can we do about it?

Well, we could stop eating at fast-food restaurants.

But what if we like fast food? What do we do then?

Maybe we could just go to fast-food restaurants that sell us the least garbage, or that recycle it.

But what if those restaurants aren't our favorites? What do we do then?

You see, it's not always easy to decide what to do. In order to save the Earth, we often have to make tough choices. But then...what other choice do we have if we really care?

Eco-Experiment #6
THINKING BEYOND

Why is it so hard for us to take care of the earth? Maybe we're so concerned with our our own lives that we just don't pay attention to other important things. This experiment will help you explore that idea.

What You'll Need
• Some friends
• A big square piece of paper (Three feet long and three feet wide would be good)
• A pencil and a small piece of paper for each person

What To Do
1. Lay the big sheet of paper on the floor. Draw lines and labels on it so it looks like the picture below.

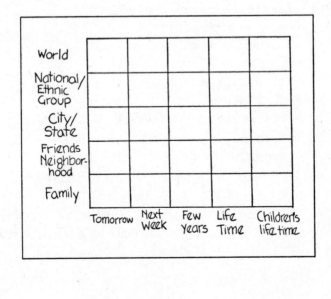

2. Ask your friends to decide when they do their "best thinking." For example: Is it in bed, just before they fall asleep? Or when they're riding their bikes? Or in the shower? When they've each figured it out, you're ready for the next step.

3. Ask your friends to close their eyes, and imagine a time last week when they were doing their "best thinking."

4. Now ask each of them to write down ten things they were thinking about doing at that time, and *when* they were thinking about doing them. For example: Were they thinking about eating dinner that night? Or seeing friends on Saturday? Or going to the movies next week?

5. It's time for the big sheet of paper.
• Everyone puts a mark in the boxes where each of their ten thoughts belongs. For example: If they were thinking about going to the movies with their friends next week, they put a mark in the box where "Next Week" and "Friends" meet. (As the drawing below shows.)

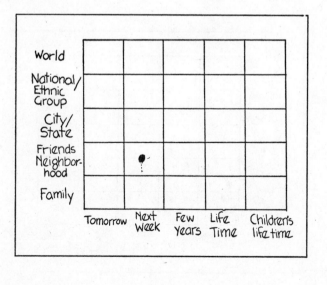

6. Now everyone should step back and take a look at where all the dots are.

What You Discover

Almost everybody's thoughts center around the things that are closest to us—our family and friends, our neighborhoods and schools, and events that will happen soon.

See how we're not used to thinking about the environment? Even if we care about saving the Earth, we hardly ever think about it. But with some practice, we can!

• We can think about the Earth while we're brushing our teeth, and turn then off the faucet to save water.

• We can think about the Earth when we want to go someplace, and then get on our bikes—or walk—instead of getting our parents to drive us in a car.

• We can turn off lights when we're not using them, knowing we're helping save energy.

• We can make the *50 Simple Things* a part of our lives just by thinking about the Earth every single day!

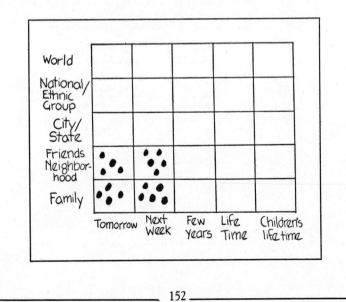

Eco-Experiment #7
MAKE YOUR OWN RECYCLED PAPER

The best way to learn how recycled paper is made is ...make it yourself! This is from First Steps in Ecology, *a book printed by the Ecology Center in Berkeley, California.*

What You'll Need
• Two and-a-half single pages from a newpaper
• A whole section of a newspaper
• A blender
• Five cups of water
• A big square pan that's at least 3 inches deep
• A piece of window screen that fits inside the pan
• A measuring cup
• A flat piece of wood the size of a newpaper's front page

What To Do

1. Tear the two and-a-half pages of newspaper into tiny pieces.

2. Drop the pieces into the blender.

3. Pour five cups of water into the blender.

4. Cover the blender (you don't want to have to scrape newspaper mush off the walls!).

5. Switch the blender on for a few seconds, or until the paper is turned into pulp.

6. Pour about one inch of water into the pan.

7. Pour the blended paper (pulp) into a measuring cup.

8. Put the screen into the pan.

9. Pour one cup of blended paper pulp over the screen.

10. Spread the pulp evenly in the water with your fingers. Feels mushy, doesn't it?

11. Lift the screen and let the water drain.

12. Open the newspaper section to the middle.

13. Place the screen with the pulp into the newspaper.

14. Close the newspaper.

15. Carefully flip over the newspaper section so the screen is on top of the pulp. This step is very important!

16. Place the board on top of the newspaper and press to squeeze out excess water.

17. Open the newspaper and take out the screen.

18. Leave the newspaper open and let the pulp dry for at least 24 hours.

19. The next day, check to make sure the pulp paper is dry.

20. If it is, carefully peel it off the newspaper.

21. Now you can use it to write on!

What You Discover

See how easy it is to make recycled paper? Now that you know how easy it is, you can help save trees and fight the garbage problem by recycling your paper...and buying recycled paper.

WRITE TO US!

This is the last page, and we like to save the last pages of all our books to tell readers our address. That way you can write and tell us what you're doing to save the Earth!

Or you can ask a question.

Or you can write and tell us some new ideas you have.

Or send us a picture. We love pictures. And stories, too.

If we gets lots of letters, we may not be able to write back to everyone. But we'll try.

Here's our address:

The Kids' EarthWorks Group
1400 Shattuck Avenue, #25
Berkeley, CA 94709

We'll look forward to hearing from you!